# Absolute Essentials of Operations Management

This short textbook consolidates all the key aspects of operations management into a concise and easily accessible reference tool.

Comprising the management of creating goods and delivering services to customers, operations management plays an essential role in the success of any organization. This book discusses the main areas of operations management, such as the design of the operations system, including product, process and job design. It also covers the management of operations, including lean operations and supply chain management.

Breaking the subject down into its key components, this book provides a core introduction for undergraduate students studying operations management as part of business and management degrees.

**Andrew Greasley** lectures in operations management and simulation modelling at Aston Business School, Birmingham, UK. He is a renowned textbook author that has taught at numerous institutions across the UK, Europe and Africa.

# Absolute Essentials of Business and Economics

Textbooks are an extraordinarily useful tool for students and teachers, as is demonstrated by their continued use in the classroom and online. Successful textbooks run into multiple editions, and in endeavouring to keep up with developments in the field, it can be difficult to avoid increasing length and complexity.

This series of shortform textbooks offers a range of books that zero in on the absolute essentials. In focusing on only the core elements of each sub-discipline, the books provide a useful alternative or supplement to traditional textbooks.

**Absolute Essentials of Green Business**
*Alan Sitkin*

**Absolute Essentials of Operations Management**
*Andrew Greasley*

For more information about this series, please visit: www.routledge.com/ Absolute-Essentials-of-Business-and-Economics/book-series/ABSOLUTE

# Absolute Essentials of Operations Management

**Andrew Greasley**

Routledge
Taylor & Francis Group

LONDON AND NEW YORK

First published 2020
by Routledge
2 Park Square, Milton Park, Abingdon, Oxon OX14 4RN

and by Routledge
52 Vanderbilt Avenue, New York, NY 10017

*Routledge is an imprint of the Taylor & Francis Group, an informa business*

*British Library Cataloguing-in-Publication Data*
A catalogue record for this book is available from the British Library

*Library of Congress Cataloging-in-Publication Data*
Names: Greasley, Andrew, author.
Title: Absolute essentials of operations management / Andrew Greasley.
Description: Milton Park, Abingdon, Oxon ; New York, NY : Routledge,
   2020. | Includes bibliographical references and index.
Identifiers: LCCN 2019036501 (print) | LCCN 2019036502 (ebook) |
   ISBN 9780367259341 (hardback) | ISBN 9780429290602 (ebook)
Subjects: LCSH: Production management. | Process control. | Project
   management. | Business logistics.
Classification: LCC TS155 .G8168 2020 (print) | LCC TS155 (ebook) |
   DDC 658.5—dc23
LC record available at https://lccn.loc.gov/2019036501
LC ebook record available at https://lccn.loc.gov/2019036502

ISBN: 978-0-367-25934-1 (hbk)
ISBN: 978-0-429-29060-2 (ebk)

Typeset in Times New Roman
by Apex CoVantage, LLC

Visit the eResources: www.routledge.com/9780367259341

# Contents

# Preface

The aim of this book is to provide a concise treatment of operations management. The book will zero in on the absolute essentials of the topic, to provide a quick and convenient guide for students. The book is designed to complement and not replace traditional textbooks that provide more in-depth coverage and offer supplementary material in the form of case studies and exercises. Operations management deals with the management of creating goods and delivering services to the customer. It thus plays an essential role in the success of any organization. The text covers the main areas of operations management, including operations strategy and the design of the operations system, including product, process and job design, and it covers the management of operations, covering topics such as lean operations and supply chain management. The target audience is undergraduates in business studies and joint degrees where no prior knowledge of the subject area is required.

# 1   Introduction

Operations management is about managing the transformation process that produces or delivers goods and services. Not every organization will have a functional department called operations, but each will undertake operations activities, because every organization produces goods and/or delivers services.

## The role of operations management

Operations management's role is to manage the transformation of an organization's inputs into finished goods and services (Figure 1.1).

The inputs to the transformation process consist of two categories of resources. Transforming resources are the inputs that undertake the transformation process on the transformed resources. The nature and mix of the transforming resources will differ between operations. The following are the two main types of transforming resources:

1   Facilities, such as buildings, equipment and process technology.
2   Staff: all the people involved in the operations process. In services, the customer may well be involved as a transforming resource. Think of a fast-food restaurant where customers are expected to order the food and take it to their table and clear up afterwards.

The transformed resources, which are the inputs acted on by the transforming resources, consist of three main types:

1   Materials: These can be transformed either physically (for example, manufacturing), by location (for example, transportation), by ownership (for example, retail) or by storage (for example, warehousing).
2   Information: This can be transformed by property (for example, by accountants), by possession (for example, market research), by storage (for example, libraries) or by location (for example, telecommunications).

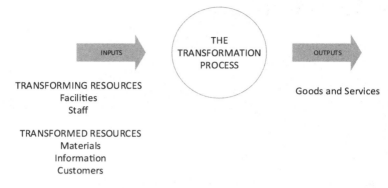

*Figure 1.1*  The role of operations management

3   Customers: They can be transformed either physically (for example, by hairdressers), by storage (for example, hotels), by location (for example, airlines), by physiological state (for example, hospitals) or by psychological state (for example, entertainment).

The transformation process will itself transform the material, information and customer resources in the way just described, in order to produce goods and services.

## The process view of operations

Three of the most important functional areas in an organization can be classified as the operations, marketing and finance functions. The marketing function works to find and create demand for the company's goods and services by understanding customer needs and developing new markets. Marketing and operations need to work closely together, because the marketing function will provide the forecast of demand from which operations can plan sufficient capacity to deliver goods and services on time. The finance function is responsible for obtaining and controlling funds and covering decisions such as investment in equipment and other operations resources such as personnel and materials. The relationship between functions can be seen as a number of subsystems within the system called the organization. Thus, each function (such as marketing) can be treated using the same input/process/output transformation model as the operations function. In other words, each function in the organization can be treated as performing an operations activity since they are transforming inputs into outputs.

This implies that every part of the organization is involved in the operations activity (to an internal or external customer), and indeed, the topic of business process management (Chapter 18) is an indication of how operations concepts are used across the organization.

## Service operations management

Because of the increased importance of services, one of the developments in operations management has been the need to integrate manufacturing and service operations to ensure that they are compatible with each other and are strategically aligned with the organization's goals. The increasing prominence of the service sector in the economies of developed countries is due to an increase in what are termed 'consumer services' and 'producer services':

- Consumer services are services aimed at the final consumers, which have risen in line with people's increasing disposable income in developed countries. Once expenditure on essentials such as food and shelter has been accounted for, people will then spend on purchases such as travel, hotels, restaurants and other social and personal services.
- Producer services are used in the production and delivery of goods and services and constitute firms providing services to other businesses, such as consultancy advice, legal advice, information technology (IT) and logistics. The rise of producer services indicates that although the share of manufacturing is declining, it still plays an important part in a nation's economy. This is because many of the producer services are actually in business to provide services to manufacturers and to other service providers. Also, many of the services that are now outsourced were once undertaken by manufacturers themselves and were thus formerly classified as part of the manufacturing sector.

There are a number of distinguishing features of services to consider.

### *Services are intangible*

Goods are tangible – they are physical things that people can touch. A service is intangible and can be seen as a process that is activated on demand. In reality, both goods and services have both tangible and intangible elements and can be placed on a continuum ranging from low to high intangibility. For example, the food in a fast-food restaurant is a major tangible element of the service. The food in a restaurant is still an important element, but other intangible elements, such as wait staff service and decor are important factors too. In fact, most operations systems produce a mixture of goods and services. Most goods have some supporting service element (for example, a maintenance contract with a new washing machine), called a facilitating service; many services have supporting goods (for example, a report provided by a management consultant), called a facilitating good.

## Services are perishable

A service is not a physical thing that can be stored but rather is a process, so often it must be consumed when it is produced or it will perish. The service availability offered by an empty room in a hotel or by an empty seat on an aircraft cannot be stored for use later. Thus, revenue lost from these unused resources can never be recovered. This would not be a problem if the demand (in terms of volume and timing) for a service could be accurately determined and service capacity provided to match this. However, this is unlikely to be the case, and unlike most goods, which can be stored if demand is lower than capacity – to be used when demand is greater than capacity – services should usually attempt to match supply with the pattern of demand.

## Services may involve the customer

Many services are produced and consumed simultaneously, which means the service provider and customer interact during the service delivery process. The amount of interaction is termed 'the degree of customer contact'. In fact, the customer is unlikely to be a passive receiver of the service but will generally be involved to a greater or lesser extent in the actual delivery of the service itself. For instance, a supermarket requires the customer to choose and transport the goods around the store and queue at an appropriate checkout till. However, it should not be assumed that all services are consumed at the point of production (for example, financial services) and that employees in a service operation have to deal directly with a customer. For the supermarket example, the checkout till is an example of high customer contact, but stores' personnel may not have to deal directly with the customer at all. A distinction in services is denoted by *back-office* tasks, which add value to the inputs of the service operation, and *front-office* tasks, which deal with the customer as both an input and an output of the operation (Figure 1.2).

Different organizations will have a different balance between front-office and back-office operations. Some traditional back-office-focused organizations, such as manufacturers, are increasing the role of service experience and thus their front-office operations. This is because they judge that the ability to differentiate the service aspect of their offering may provide a

*Figure 1.2* Front office and back office in operations management

longer-term source of competitive advantage than they can achieve by differentiating the goods themselves. Some other organizations, however, are moving in the opposite direction by recognizing that the tangible aspect of the service package delivered by back-office operations is adding customer value. For example, budget airlines have eliminated many front-line service aspects of the flight experience and focused on the transportation of customer process itself.

## *Servitization*

In general, manufacturers offer services to some extent (for example, a maintenance contract offered with equipment) but often compete on a strategy based on their products in terms of product innovation and product cost reduction. Servitization represents a process that enables manufacturing companies to move to a service-led competitive strategy. This entails viewing the manufacturer as a service provider and enhancing the traditional manufacturing strategy built around product-based innovation with one that aims to improve their customer processes. Advanced services are a special case of servitization, which involves the manufacturer offering contracts to customers that encompass payment based on the performance of a product over an extended period of time. Advanced services are delivered by product-service systems (PSS) (Baines and Lightfoot, 2013), in which the manufacturer provides a capability to undertake a process for the customer. This capability can entail choosing suitable equipment and consumables, monitoring performance and undertaking maintenance and disposal. The manufacturer receives payment for the capability that is used by the customer.

## Operations management and environmental sustainability

Operations managers need to consider how their actions affect the world's natural environment. These issues can range from conserving water supplies;

polluting the land, sea and air; and limiting carbon emissions that lead to global warming. Thus, operations should design and manage the transformation process to minimize energy use in both the process and through the lifecycle of the product or service itself. Transportation methods employed should also seek to reduce the carbon footprint through less journey time or more environmentally friendly transportation methods.

## Reference

Baines, T. and Lightfoot, H. (2013) *Made to Serve: How manufacturers can compete through servitization and product-service systems*, John Wiley & Sons Ltd.

# 2 Operations strategy

Operations management can provide the basis for a firm's competitive strategy. The purpose of an operations strategy is to interpret the overall business strategy, which will be concerned with goals such as growth and profitability, into goals that direct how operations will be managed. These goals may be defined by the five operations performance objectives: quality, speed, dependability, flexibility and cost. This chapter will formulate a strategy to achieve these goals, one that is concerned with matching internal operations capability with external competitive market requirements.

## The role of operations strategy

Hayes and Wheelwright (1988) assert that the success of organizations depends on their overall operations capability and so provide a model that enables managers to identify operations' current strategic role and the changes needed to increase competitiveness. The four-stage model traces the contribution of the operations function from a largely reactive role in stage 1 to a proactive element in competitive success in stage 4.

### Stage 1: internal neutrality

Here the operations' function has little to contribute to competitive success and is seen as a barrier to better competitive performance by other functions. The operations function is simply attempting to reach a minimum acceptable standard required by the rest of the organization while avoiding any major mistakes – hence the term 'internal neutrality'. However, a major mistake by operations could still entail serious consequences for the rest of the organization (for example, product recall).

### Stage 2: external neutrality

Here the operations' function begins to focus on comparing its performance with competitor organizations. Although it may not be innovative enough to be in the first division of companies in its market, by taking the best ideas and attempting to match the performance of competitors, it is attempting to be externally neutral.

### Stage 3: internally supportive

Here the operations' function is one of the best in its market area and aspires to be the best in its market. The operations function will thus be organizing and developing the operations capabilities to meet the strategic requirements of the organization. Operations is taking a role in the implementation of strategy and being *internally* supportive.

### Stage 4: externally supportive

Here the operations' function is becoming central to strategy making and is providing the foundation for future competitive success. This may be delivered by organizing resources in ways that are innovative and capable of adapting as markets change. When operations is in the role of the long-term driver of strategy, it is being *externally* supportive.

As the organization moves from stage 1 to stage 4, its role moves from being reactive in response to strategic objectives passed down to it, to ensuring resources are developed to support the strategy, to (in stage 4) providing the business with its competitive advantage.

## The performance objectives of operations management

The five performance objectives (Slack et al., 2016) allow the organization to measure its operations' performance in achieving its strategic goals:

1   Quality.
2   Speed.
3   Dependability.
4   Flexibility.
5   Cost.

Each of these objectives will be discussed according to how it is measured and its significance to organizational competitiveness.

### Quality

Quality covers both the quality of the design of the product or service itself and the quality of the process that delivers the product or service. From a customer perspective, quality characteristics include reliability, performance and aesthetics. From an operations viewpoint, quality is related to how closely the product or service meets the specification required by the design, termed 'the quality of conformance'. The advantages of good quality on competitiveness include increased dependability, with fewer problems due to poor quality; reduced costs, by avoiding expenditure on defective products and services; and improved customer service, leading to high customer satisfaction.

## Speed

Speed is the time delay between a customer requesting a product or service and their receiving that product or service. Although making a product in advance by the use of a make-to-stock system may reduce the delivery time as seen by the customer, it cannot be used for services. This approach also risks the product becoming obsolete and ties up the cost of any stock in working capital. An advantage of speed is that it can be used to both reduce costs (by eliminating the costs associated with make-to-stock systems) and reduce delivery time, leading to better customer service.

## Dependability

Dependability can be measured by the percentage of customers that receive a product or service within the delivery time promised. In some instances, it may even be important to deliver not too quickly, but only at the time required (for example, a consignment of wet concrete for construction). Dependability leads to better customer service when the customer can trust that the product or service will be delivered when expected. Dependability can also lead to lower cost, in that progress checking and other activities designed to ensure things happen on time can be reduced in the organization.

## Flexibility

Flexibility is the ability of the organization to change what it does. Flexibility is needed so that the organization can adapt to changing customer needs in terms of product range and varying demand and to cope with capacity shortfalls due to equipment breakdown or component shortage. The following types of flexibility can be identified:

- Product or service – to be able to introduce new product or services.
- Mix – to be able to change the proportion (mix) between the different products or services offered.

- Volume – to be able to decrease or increase overall product/service output.
- Delivery – to be able to change the timing of a delivery.

Flexibility can be measured in terms of range (the amount of the change) and response (the speed of the change). The range and response dimensions are connected in the sense that the more something is changed (range), the longer it will take (response). In general, the benefit of flexibility from the customer's point of view is that it means that the organisation is able to adapt to customer needs.

### *Cost*

Cost is considered to be the finances required to obtain the inputs (transforming and transformed resources) and manage the transformation process that produces finished goods and services. If an organization is competing on price, then it must keep its cost base lower than the competition's. Then it will either make more profit than rivals if the price is equal or gain market share if price is lower. Improvements in the other four performance objectives can also lead to a reduction in cost.

## Operations strategy formulation

The Hill method (Hill and Hill, 2018) proposes that the issue of the degree of 'fit' between the proposed marketing strategy and the operation's ability to support it is resolved at the business level by meeting corporate (strategic) objectives. Thus, Hill provides an iterative framework that links the corporate objectives (which provide the organizational direction), the marketing strategy (which defines how the organization will compete in its chosen markets) and the operations strategy (which provides the capability to compete in those markets).

The framework consists of five steps.

### *Step 1: corporate objectives*

Corporate objectives provide a direction for the organization and performance indicators, which allow progress in achieving those objectives to be measured. The objectives depend on the needs of external and internal stakeholders and thus include financial measures such as profit and growth rates and employee practices such as skills development and appropriate environmental policies.

### Step 2: marketing strategy

A marketing strategy to meet the corporate objectives defined involves identifying target markets and deciding how to compete in these markets. This requires using product/service characteristics such as range, mix and volume that the operations activity are required to provide. Other issues considered are the level of innovation and product development and the choice of 'leader' or 'follower' strategies in the chosen markets.

### Step 3: how does one qualify and win orders in the marketplace?

This translates the marketing strategy into a range of competitive factors (for example, price, quality, delivery speed) on which the product or service wins orders. Customers will value a range of competitive factors for any particular product/service; thus, it is necessary to identify the relative importance of a range of factors. Hill distinguishes between the following types of competitive factors that relate to securing customer orders in the marketplace:

- *Order-winning factors* are factors that contribute to winning business from customers. They are key reasons that customers purchase the goods or services, and raising the performance of the order-winning factor may secure more business.
- *Qualifying factors* are factors that must be considered to earn business from customers. The performance of qualifying factors must be at a certain level to gain business from customers, but performance above this level will not necessarily gain further competitive advantage.

While it may be necessary to raise performance on some (qualifying) factors to a certain level in order to be considered by the customer, a further rise in the level of performance may not achieve an increase in competitiveness. Instead competitiveness may then depend on raising the level of performance of different order-winning factors higher than those of competitors. Because it is more difficult to raise performance to the best-in-class than it is to be considered in the race, it is the order-winning competitive factors that should be translated into the internal performance objectives that the organization must excel at. For example, an order winner of fast delivery should be translated into the performance objective of speed, a wide product range translated to mix flexibility and low price translated to cost.

### Steps 4 and 5: delivery system choice (structural decisions) and infrastructure choice (infrastructural decisions)

Steps 4 and 5 of Hill's method involve putting the processes and resources in place that provide the required performance as defined by the performance objectives. Hill categorizes operations decision areas into delivery system choice, which is often referred to as structural decisions, and infrastructure choice, commonly called infrastructural decisions.

Delivery system choice, also referred to as structural decisions, concerns aspects of the organization's physical resources, such as service delivery systems and capacity provision. These elements may be expensive and difficult to change quickly and so provide the basic capability of the operations system. Structural decisions include the choice of process type implemented in manufacturing (project, jobbing, batch, line or continuous) or services (professional, shop, mass) and the associated layout types. Further decisions involve capacity issues, including the volume, timing and location of capacity provision and the provision of process technology for materials, information and customers.

Infrastructural decisions describe the systems, policies and practices that determine how the structural elements covered in step 4 are managed. Structural decisions determine the overall capability of the operations system, but infrastructure elements determine how much of this capability is realized. Infrastructural decisions include the management of the product and service design process, the management of organizational processes, the design of jobs, the management of capacity, the scheduling of operations, inventory management, planning and control systems, such as just-in-time (JIT) and enterprise resource planning (ERP); supply chain management; and project management. Performance improvement and performance measurement systems are also included under this heading.

## References

Hayes, R.H., and Wheelwright, S.C. (1988) *Restoring Our Competitive Edge: Competing Through Manufacturing*, John Wiley & Sons, Ltd.

Hill, A., and Hill, T. (2018) *Operations Strategy: Design, Implementation and Delivery*, Red Globe Press.

Slack, N., Brandon-Jones, A., and Johnston, R. (2016) *Operations Management*, 8th edn., Pearson Education Limited.

# 3    Process types

When designing the transformation process that delivers goods or services, we need to consider the volume and variety of the product or service that the organisation provides. Volume and variety are related, so we can generally consider that companies serve their customers on a continuum from a combination of low-volume/high-variety products and services to high-volume/low-variety products and services. Along this continuum, we will define general process configurations called process types for manufacturing and services

## Manufacturing process types

There are five categories of manufacturing process types, which are placed along the volume/variety continuum, as in Figure 3.1, and they will now be considered.

### *Project*

These are used for low-volume, high-variety products and have the following characteristics:

- They are one-off products to a customer specification.
- The location of the project is stationary, and transforming resources move to the location of the project.
- They require the coordination of many individuals and activities.
- They demand a problem-solving approach, to ensure that they are completed on time.
- They require a comparatively long duration to manufacture.
- Resources such as staff and equipment are often dedicated to a project during its duration.

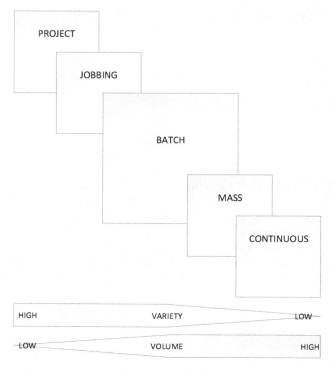

*Figure 3.1* Manufacturing process types

Examples of using a project process include building construction, movie film production and custom-built furniture.

### *Jobbing*

These are used for low-volume, high-variety products and have the following characteristics:

*   They are used to make a one-off (or low-volume) product to a customer specification.
*   The product moves to the location of transforming resources.
*   Resources such as staff and equipment are shared between many products.
*   They can use skilled labour in order to cope with the need for customization (variety).

Examples of the use of a jobbing process include custom tailors and a return-and-repair shop.

### Batch

These are used for medium-volume, medium-variety products and have the following characteristics:

- They cover a wide range of volume and variety combinations.
- A batch is a group of products that are processed together. The batch (group) size can range from two to hundreds of products.
- These products move to the location of transforming resources.
- The setting up of machinery occurs between batches.
- They sometimes use specialized labour and equipment dedicated to certain batches.
- Queues of work may dramatically increase the time that the product takes to move through the process.

Examples of the use of a batch process include vehicle component assembly, clothing manufacture and bakeries.

### Mass

These are used for high-volume, low-variety products and have the following characteristics:

- Although there may be variants in the product design, the production process will essentially be the same for all the products.
- High volumes mean that it is cost-effective to use specialized labour and equipment.
- The movement of the product may be automated using a conveyor system.
- The production process is broken down into a number of small, simple tasks.
- To ensure a smooth flow of product, the process times per unit is equalized at each production stage.
- The setting up of equipment is minimized and the use of equipment is high.

Examples of the use of a mass process include vehicle manufacturing and the assembly of consumer durables such as televisions and computers.

### Continuous

These are used for high-volume, low-variety products and have the following characteristics:

- The products produced by a continuous operation are usually a continuous flow, such as oil, gas and electricity.
- They use a large amount of specialized and dedicated equipment.
- They are often in constant operation, 24 hours a day.
- The role of labour in the operation of the processes is mainly one of monitoring and controlling the process equipment, with little contact with the product.

Examples of a continuous process include an oil refinery, electricity production and steelmaking.

A key issue in manufacturing is that process type decisions can take a relatively large amount of time and money to implement, whereas market needs in a competitive environment can change rapidly. The project and jobbing process types imply a wide variety of outputs, which will require meeting market requirements for design and innovation. The batch process type covers a wide range of volume and variety outputs, so to ensure strategic focus, the organisation needs to distinguish between batch towards the jobbing end of the continuum and batch towards the mass end of the volume/variety continuum. Mass and continuous process types imply selling a narrow range of standard products in high volumes.

## Service process types

There are three categories of service process types (Figure 3.2) that will now be considered.

### Professional service

These are low-volume, high-variety services and have the following characteristics:

- They have high levels of customization in that each service delivery will be tailored to meet individual customer needs.
- They have high levels of customer contact and a relatively high proportion of staff supplying the service in relation to customers.
- They emphasize delivering a process rather than a tangible product associated with a process.

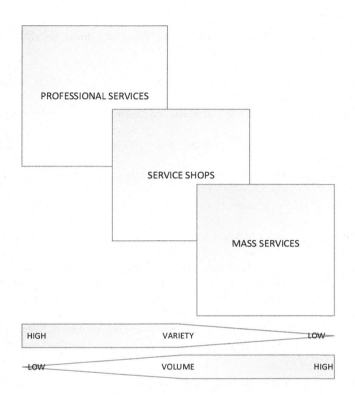

*Figure 3.2* Service process types

Examples of a professional service include management consultancy, doctors and health and safety inspectors.

### Service shop

These are mid-volume, mid-variety services and have the following characteristics:

- They have a mix of staff and equipment used to deliver the service.
- They emphasize both the service delivery process itself and any tangible items that are associated with the service.

Examples of service shops include banks, restaurants and travel agencies.

*Mass service*

These are high-volume, low-variety services and have the following characteristics:

• They offer little customization for the service to individual customer needs.
• They offer limited contact between the customer and people providing the service.
• Equipment will be used to improve the efficiency of the service delivery process.
• They emphasize the tangible item associated with the service delivery.

Examples of mass service providers are supermarkets, rail services and airports.

As in manufacturing, in services a key issue in process type choice is that process decisions can take a relatively large amount of time and money to implement, whereas market needs in a competitive environment can change rapidly. The professional process type implies a wide variety of outputs, which will require meeting market requirements for design and innovation. The service process type covers a middle ground of volume and variety, so it has a limited amount of customisation during service delivery. Mass services process types imply selling a narrow range of standard services.

## Matching process type to volume and variety

For a certain volume and variety combination, an organization needs to make a choice regarding which process type to use. In Figure 3.3, the example volume and variety position shown by the vertical dashed line intersects with the diagonal 'line of fit' for the process types, which indicates the use of a batch process type in this case.

Thus, if a jobbing process type was used in the volume and variety position shown in Figure 3.3, then operations would have too much flexibility for the amount of variety required and thus higher costs than another producer supplying the same market using a batch process type. Likewise, if a mass process type were used in this position, then the operation would have too little flexibility for the amount of variety required. And thus, they would have higher costs than another producer supplying the same market using a batch process type. This is due to the high changeover costs that they would incur in moving from one product to another to meet the required variety of outputs required by the market. This concept can also be related to matching the volume and variety of service processes by using Figure 3.2.

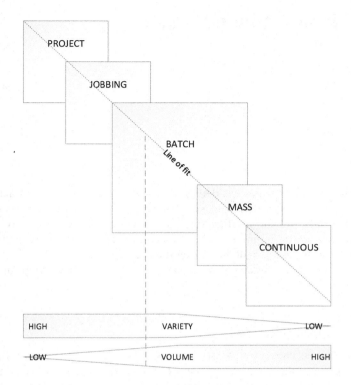

*Figure 3.3* Matching process type to volume and variety

# 4   Process layout types

The process layout concerns determining the physical location of activities in the transformation process to ensure an efficient flow of customers, materials and information through the operations system. Physical layout may not be important for information activities but is relevant in manufacturing facilities and services such as administrative activities for the design of office layouts that can facilitate teamwork among groups of people.

## Process layout types

There are four categories of process layout types: fixed position, functional, cell and line, which are placed along the volume/variety continuum. Although the main layout types can be adapted to meet the needs of a particular manufacturing or service system, it may be the case that a mix of layout types is required in a single operation. For example, hospitals are basically a functional layout with people with similar needs (for example, intensive care) grouped together. However, the layout also shows characteristics of a fixed-position layout in that staff, medicines and equipment are brought to the location of the customer. Layout type choice is strategic because it can represent a large amount of capital investment in equipment and workforce and so sets a constraint around which the company can compete. The layout type choice is linked to the process type choice, but as can be seen from Figure 4.1, there may be more than one layout type which corresponds with a particular process type. In this case, the choice will depend on the characteristics of the layout type that are particularly relevant for the product or service to be delivered. The layout types and their associated process types are shown in Figure 4.1 and will now be considered.

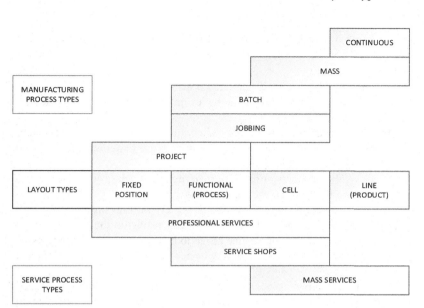

*Figure 4.1* Process layout types and their relationship to process types

### *Fixed-position layout*

The fixed-position layout is used for low-volume, high-variety products and services and has the following characteristics:

- It is used when the product or service does not move, so the process takes place at the location of product creation or service delivery.
- All resources for producing the product or service, such as staff, must move to the location of the product or service.
- It emphasizes the scheduling and coordination of resources to ensure that they are available in the required amounts at the required time. For example, in a restaurant, the order needs to be taken and food delivered to the table at the appropriate time.
- Process types associated with a fixed-position layout are the project process type in manufacturing and the professional service type in services.

Examples of fixed-position layouts include construction sites such as for buildings or for large ships, aircraft manufacture and full-service restaurants.

### Functional layout

The functional layout is used for mid-volume, mid-variety products and services and has the following characteristics:

- A functional layout is also called a process layout.
- It is one in which resources that have similar functions or processes are grouped together.
- It is used when there is a large variety among the products or services being delivered and when it may not be feasible to dedicate facilities to each individual product or service.
- It allows the products or customers to move to each group of resources in turn, on the basis of their individual requirements.
- In service systems, they allow a wide variety of routes through the process that may be chosen by customers depending on their needs.
- It allows the product or service range to be extended, and as long as no new resources are required, it may be accommodated within the current layout.
- The process types associated with a functional layout are the project, jobbing and batch process types in manufacturing and professional services and service shops in services.

Examples of functional layouts include supermarkets, hospitals, department stores and component manufacturers.

### Cell layout

The cell layout is used for mid-volume, mid-variety products and services and has the following characteristics:

- This layout attempts to combine the efficiency of a line layout with the flexibility of a functional layout.
- It is created from putting together resources that service a subset (called a family) of the total range of products or services.
- The routing of products and services is simplified by processing in a single cell, reducing transportation time between locations.
- The procedure used to group products or services to create a family is called group technology.
- It offers the opportunity for automation due to the proximity of the process stages.
- It can lead to extra expenditure due to the extra resources required when implementing cells.

- The process types associated with a cell layout are jobbing; batch and mass process types in manufacturing and professional services; service shops; and mass services in services.

Examples of cell layouts include custom manufacture, a maternity unit in a hospital and a cafeteria with several serving areas. In services, a cell layout could involve an insurance company organized by types of claims (such as car, home or travel).

*Group technology*

The process of grouping products or services to create a family is called group technology. Group technology has three aspects:

1   Grouping parts or customers into families. This aims to reduce the change-over time between batches, allowing smaller batch sizes and thus improving flexibility. Parts or customers can be grouped together according to factors such as processing similarity.
2   Grouping physical facilities into cells. This aims to reduce transportation time between processes. Material and customer movement is restricted to within the cell, and throughput times are therefore reduced. Cells can be U-shaped to allow workers to work at more than one process while minimizing movement.
3   Creating groups of multi-skilled workers. This enables increased autonomy and flexibility on the part of operators, which can lead to easier changeovers from one part to another and which increases job enrichment for members of the group. This in turn can improve motivation and have a beneficial effect on quality.

**Line layout**

This is used for high-volume, low-variety products and services and has the following characteristics:

- A line layout is also called a product layout.
- It arranges the resources required for a product or service around the needs of that product or service.
- In manufacturing applications, such as assembly lines with a high volume of a standard product, the products will move in a flow from one processing station to the next.
- In services, the requirements of a specific group of customers are identified and resources set up sequentially so that the customers flow

through the system, moving from one stage to another until the service has been completed.

- Stages in the assembly line or flow line must be *balanced*. This means that the time spent by components or customers should be approximately the same for each stage; otherwise, queues will form at the slowest stage.
- It is an efficient delivery system in that the use of dedicated equipment in a balanced line will allow a fast throughput time.
- If any stage of the line fails, then in effect, the output from the whole line is lost, so it lacks a robustness to a loss of resources (for example, equipment failure or staff illness).
- The process types associated with a line layout are mass and continuous process types in manufacturing and mass services in services.

Examples of line layouts include car assembly, self-service cafes, car valeting, golf courses and assembly lines.

# 5  Facility design
## Supply, capacity and location

Facility design is taken here to refer to decisions regarding how capacity will be supplied by the organization to meet market demand. There are three main issues involved in decisions regarding this area. Supply network design concerns how the organization's facilities be configured; long-term capacity-planning concerns how much capacity should be supplied; and facility location concerns where the capacity will be located.

## Supply network design

A generic supply network is shown in Figure 5.1, which can be defined as the configuration of the organization's relationship with its suppliers and the choice about what activities the organization should undertake internally and what should be subcontracted to other agencies. Note that although the flow of material is shown from left to right (downstream), there will be a flow of information in the opposite direction (upstream) between organizations in the supply network. Managing this flow of information upstream is a major element of supply network management. The terms 'supply network' and 'supply chain' are often used interchangeably, but here the supply chain is taken to mean one of a series of linkages within the supply network.

Supply networks can improve delivery and cost performance relative to fixed supply facilities in that the network can pool demand and increase volume to reduce costs and choose different facilities to provide products for a given customer under different conditions. A network should lead to a more robust system that avoids capacity bottlenecks by using close coordination facilitated by the use of communications technology. The configuration of the supply network will become more complex as we move from a home operations configuration through to a global operated organization.

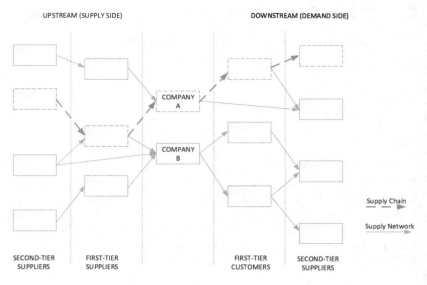

UPSTREAM (SUPPLY SIDE)                    DOWNSTREAM (DEMAND SIDE)

COMPANY
A

COMPANY
B

Supply Chain

Supply Network

SECOND-TIER        FIRST-TIER              FIRST-TIER        SECOND-TIER
SUPPLIERS          SUPPLIERS               CUSTOMERS         SUPPLIERS

*Figure 5.1*  A supply network

## 1  Home operations

In this configuration, all supplies of goods and services are made from within the home country, and demand from other countries is made by direct export. This strategy enables control of operations in a familiar environment and can provide economies of scale and scope advantages by focusing output in one location. The disadvantages of this approach include the difficulty in meeting variations in customer needs in different overseas markets, the difficulty in providing prompt and reliable delivery over extended distances and the loss of markets where face-to-face services are required.

## 2  Multi-domestic operations

This approach configures operations facilities in each country where the organization operates. This provides a relatively straightforward operations control and allows products and services to be tailored to meet local demands. The disadvantages of this approach include the cost of establishing multiple operations and the potential loss of economies of scale and scope in operating in this way.

## 3 Regional operations

In this configuration, operations is divided into regions (such as Europe), with each region being served by a self-contained operations facility configuration. This is an attempt both to enable a degree of customization of product and service to meet local needs and to obtain economies of scale and scope across the region.

## 4 Global operations

In global organizations the aim is to create a network of operations that will sell the same products in several countries, increase overall sales thereby reducing the cost per unit of development, coordinate the work of subsidiaries to provide a product/service to the global customer and shift production in response to exchange-rate fluctuations.

## Long-term capacity planning

The long-term capacity plan is a key determinant of the competitiveness of an organization. Capacity must be available at the time needed and in the current format to ensure that targets are met. There will also be constraints on overall capacity caused by the scarcity of certain types of capacity (such as employee skills). Thus, the availability of different types of capacity must be considered in order to avoid bottlenecks. This section will consider long-term capacity-planning issues in terms of capacity volume and capacity timing.

### Capacity volume

In determining the optimum capacity level for a facility, the concepts of economies of scale and economies of scope are considered.

Economies of scale relate to the capital costs of building a new facility and the fixed costs of operating a facility. As a facility is expanded and fixed costs remain the same, the average cost of producing each unit will fall until the best operating level of the facility is reached and the lowest average unit cost met. Past a certain point, however, diseconomies of scale occur and average unit costs rise. This is due to the required capacity output of the facility being higher than it has been designed for, and operating at this level can cause a loss of efficiency from factors such as the complexity of combining many products and services; the extensive use of (relatively expensive) shift working and overtime; and decreased staff morale due to poor working conditions.

Economies of scope are created by the ability to produce many products in one highly flexible production facility more cheaply than in separate facilities. In terms of service operations, this means serving many customer groups from one facility. An example is outsourced call centre operations, which use specialist firms to serve many clients by using Internet technology.

### Capacity timing

An organization can adopt three main approaches to ensuring the correct amount of capacity is available at the right time to meet future plans: lead capacity, match capacity and lag capacity.

A lead capacity policy, also called an aggressive expansion approach, aims to obtain extra capacity above forecast demand and so try to ensure that capacity is sufficient if demand increases above what was forecast. This has the advantage of helping to maintain high levels of customer service and responding quickly to increases in customer demand but has the disadvantage of the cost of maintaining the excess capacity for all the different types of capacity (people, equipment, locations) required over time. The amount of excess capacity, which can be calculated as the percentage of capacity that is not used on average, is called the capacity cushion.

A match capacity policy simply means obtaining sufficient capacity to match forecast demand. The advantage of this option is that it avoids the costs of a capacity cushion and instead uses strategies such as outsourcing, which can quickly fill capacity shortfalls. The disadvantage is the difficulty of forecasting future demand accurately enough in order that capacity can be obtained at the right time to meet that demand. Long project lead times for investments in capacity, such as infrastructure projects means demand forecasts, have to project further into the future and so are prone to greater error.

A lag capacity strategy, also termed a 'wait-and-see approach', is to add capacity only when extra demand is present that would use the additional resources. This has the advantage of delaying investments until it is certain that they are needed and ensures a high use of the capacity acquired. However, this option may mean customers are lost as they move to competitor products and services before the additional capacity is in place. This strategy may also incur a loss of flexibility as a consequence of the continual high use of resources.

## Facility location

The facility location is strategic as it can have a large impact on the investment in the operation's resources and also on the operation's market performance. A wrong location can lead to an inability to configure suitable resources for a resource-based strategy and could also mean competitive factors cannot be met. Services are generally classified as back office and front office, where back-office services do not require customer contact and thus provide more flexibility in the location decision. Front-office services, however, require customer contact, but when making the location decision, it is useful to distinguish them by the nature of the movement of user (customer) and provider of the service.

Separated services provide a service directly to a customer so can be classified as front-office but do not actually require either the user or provider to physically come together to enable the service to take place. Call centres have been established internationally that provide services to customers at a distance.

Demander-located services require the service provider to move to the location of the customer. An example is management consultancy, where it would usually be expected that the service provider would be present at least in part at the premises of the client. On the other hand, provider-located services require the user to move to the location of the service provider, which they may have to do to access specialist resources and staff – such as at a hospital or as a feature of a service, as in a hotel.

Peripatetic services involve both customer and provider moving to the location of the service encounter. Trade shows and conferences fall under this category.

### *Supply-side and demand-side influences on facility location*

The location decision must consider factors that vary in such a way as to influence cost as location varies (supply-side factors) and factors that vary in such a way as to influence customer service as location varies (demand-side factors). In service organizations, a need for customer contact may mean that demand-side influences will dominate, whereas in a manufacturing, company labour and distribution costs may mean that supply-side influences dominate.

Supply-side influences include distribution and transportation costs, which can be considerable, especially for a manufacturing organization that deals in tangible products. The sheer volume of the raw material involved in operations such as steel production means that a location decision will tend to favour areas near to raw materials. A manufacturer and seller of custom-built furniture, however, will need to be near potential customers. For service companies, the need to be in a market-oriented location means that the cost of transportation of goods will not be a major factor in the location decision. However, many service organizations need to distribute stock from warehouses whose location should be considered carefully. Distribution across country borders means that a whole series of additional costs and delays must be taken into account, including import duties and delays in moving freight between different transportation methods. A site near to an airport or a rail link to an airport may be an important factor if delivery speed is important. Labour costs have generally become less important as the proportion of direct labour cost in high-volume manufacturing has fallen. What is becoming more important is the skills and flexibility of the labour force to adapt to new working methods and to engage in continuous improvement efforts. The wage rate of labour can be a factor in location decisions, especially when the service can be provided easily in alternative locations. Both the cost of the land and the cost of purchasing materials and then building a facility are directly related to the location decision. These costs should be considered together since low-cost land may require substantial preparation to make it suitable for building development. Finally, there are a number of factors that are not financial but may have an effect on the location decision. These include the potential for objections to development on environmental grounds, local regulations regarding business developments and the necessary quality of life in the area needed to attract skilled employees.

Demand-side influences include the need for a pool of skilled labour is becoming increasingly important. Location image may also be important, with retail outlets in particular wishing to locate in an area that 'fits' with the image they are trying to project. Shopping districts will often be associated with a particular type of retail outlet, such as designer clothing. Finally, for many service organizations in particular, the location of the facility must be convenient for the potential customer. This includes restaurants, where customers may be prepared to travel a short distance, and hospitals, where the speed of response is vital to the service. The physical link between customer and service provider can be in either direction. For example, household goods such as gas ovens and central heating boilers will be serviced by staff at the customer's home.

# 6 Process technology

Process technology is an important aspect of operations in that it has led to a large growth in productivity in both manufacturing, where the emphasis is on technology for material and information transformation, and services, where the emphasis is on technology for information and customer transformations. Process technology can be used to enhance performance along performance objectives such as improving delivery speed and increasing quality.

## Process technology for materials

This section will describe some of the software systems and hardware technologies that have had a widespread impact on manufacturing firms.

### Software systems

Computer-aided design (CAD) is one of the most widespread technologies, used in even relatively small firms. A CAD system allows the designer to create drawings on a computer screen to assist in the visual design of a product or service. The drawings can be viewed from any angle, and drawings can be zoomed in to allow users to inspect a design in detail. Drawings are held in a database for future use and dissemination between designers and engineers all across the company. Computer-aided process planning (CAPP) extends CAD by transmitting a process plan of how parts will be manufactured to the machine tool – for example, deciding on how individual pieces are to be cut from a sheet of metal. CAPP systems can also sequence parts through a number of process steps. Computer-aided engineering (CAE) takes the drawings in a CAD system and subjects the designs to simulated tests. For example, the behaviour of an engineering design for elements of a bridge can be observed under various amounts of stress. This allows various design options to be tested quickly and cheaply.

### Hardware technologies

Computer numerically controlled (CNC) machines are machine tools that can be controlled by computer. Automated material handling systems (AMH) are designed to improve efficiency in the movement, storage and retrieval of materials. Types of systems include automated guided vehicle (AGV) systems that transport material on driverless vehicles to various locations in the plant. Automated storage and retrieval systems (AS/RS) handle the storage and retrieval of materials by using computers to direct automatic loaders to pick and place items in a storage facility. Flexible manufacturing cell (FMC) systems integrate individual items of automation described earlier to form an automated manufacturing system. Flexible manufacturing systems (FMS) extend the facilities of an FMC by incorporating automatic parts loading and unloading facilities and an AGV system for parts movement. When these technologies are integrated by using a computer network and database system, the resulting automated system is called computer-integrated manufacture (CIM). CIM is a fully integrated system: the areas of design, testing, fabrication, assembly, inspection and material handling are automated and integrated by using technology. Autonomous robots can learn, adapt, and evolve by using capabilities like machine learning and computer vision. For example, robots equipped with gyroscopes and accelerometers, along with an on-board camera and laser scanner can tell how and where they are moving, and they 'know' what tasks they are capable of covering. The robots can then autonomously evaluate a task, divide it between themselves and collaborate to complete it. For example, when an individual robot reaches the end of its battery charge, it will transmit its position to a fully charged unit that can take over while it recharges.

## Process technology for information

Three types of information system considered here are e-business, e-commerce, m-business, the IoT and Industry 4.0.

### E-business

E-business can be seen as the transformation of business processes through the use of Internet technologies. E-business opportunities can be classified by whether an organization is using the Internet to transact with consumers, called business-to-consumer (B2C) or other businesses, called business-to-business (B2B). B2B transactions predominate over the Internet in terms of value if not frequency. The benefits of e-business for operations relate to areas such as supply chain integration using B2B and B2C interactions as well as the increased efficiency and effectiveness of internal business processes using employee-to-employee (E2E) interactions.

## E-commerce

E-commerce can be considered to be all electronically mediated transactions between an organization and any third party that it deals with. By this definition, non-financial transactions such as customer requests for further information would also be considered to be part of e-commerce. Buy-side e-commerce refers to transactions to procure resources needed by an organization from its suppliers. Sell-side e-commerce refers to transactions involved in selling products to an organization's customers.

## M-business

M-business can be defined as the integration of Internet and wireless communications technology. It is a result of mobile communications facilitated by broadband (high-bandwidth) Internet connections and wireless technology (for example, mobile phones using radio waves). One m-business technology is radio frequency identification (RFID) systems, which consist of a tag that can be attached to an item. The tag contains a microchip, which contains information about the item, and its location is transmitted upon request by using radio signals to an RFID reader. The RFID readers then transmit this information, using a wired or wireless connection, to a computer network. The system uses a short-range radio system for receiving the information from the tag but does not require a direct line of sight that, for example, a barcode system requires.

## Internet of Things (IoT)

The IoT can refer to the use of the Internet as a network to enable connection and communication between objects with embedded sensors. A primary driver of the IoT is the broad deployment of sensors that are smaller, cheaper and more powerful than they used to be. There are many applications of the IoT, including in manufacturing the use for real-time monitoring of production processes to allow early correction of errors and increased efficiency – for example, to improve visibility in the manufacturing supply chain. Other applications include the use of data streamed from delivery vehicles to schedule maintenance activities outside of operating hours and customer tracking devices that can be used to present targeted promotions to customers as they move through a store.

***Industry 4.0***

Industry 4.0 is based on the idea of a fully integrated manufacturing industry. The term is also referred to as the Fourth Industrial Revolution, enabled by digital transformation and the integration of IT and automation systems in manufacturing. A major element of Industry 4.0 is cyber-physical systems (CPS) that allow the physical components in an industrial process, such as machines, workers and robots, to be integrated into the virtual network of the IoT. The goal is to have embedded computers and networks monitor and control the physical processes and enable information to be shared at the different stages of creating and manufacturing a product. This will enable the establishment of a self-adapting production system based on transparency of information and predictive power. Further key elements to Industry 4.0 are thus the infrastructure to store and manage the big data generated by CPS and the use of analytics to provide the predictive analysis required.

## Process technology for customers

One approach to improving service delivery is to use process technology in the service delivery process itself. In an active customer-technology interaction such as an automated teller machine (ATM) at a bank, the technology can enable customers to avail themselves of the service at a time of their choosing and to make choices regarding that service. From a service provider viewpoint, this has the advantage of reducing staffing requirements and empowering customers by giving them a greater sense of control over the type of service they require. However, customers have different preferences, and many facilities may well need both customer-driven and traditional people-based service delivery systems such as a call centre or physical outlet. Process technology also exists for passive customer-technology interactions such as transportation systems – for example, moving walkways for directing people at an airport or an underground tube system in a city. Because of the lack of interaction between the customer and technology, customers will need clear instructions on how to use the technology, to avoid confusion. In a supported customer-technology interaction, there is a human server who acts as an intermediary between the customer and the technology itself. This means that advice and guidance can be given to the customer by the server in making their choices. Some organizations encourage their customers to use active rather than supported technology, to reduce staffing costs. For example, many airlines charge customers extra if they wish to check in at the airport rather than undertake the task online.

# Choosing process technology

In terms of operations management, investing in process technology is a strategic decision in that it helps the organization meet the requirements of the market in which it is competing. In particular, IT investments can be sees as a bridge between the external business environment and internal business processes. In general, investments in processing technology should be used to enhance performance along the key performance objectives identified in the strategy process, such as improving delivery speed and increasing quality. It is also important that the form of the technology investment match the volume/variety requirements of the task and provide the appropriate trade-off between flexibility and cost. To assist the process technology decision, we consider three characteristics of process technology that vary with volume and variety, namely scale, automation and integration (Slack et al., 2016).

## *Scale of the technology*

The scale refers to the capacity of individual units of process technology. In general terms, we have a choice about whether we make up our capacity with a few high-volume units or many low-volume units. Large-scale units of technology will generally have a high capital cost but a low operating-unit cost and thus help achieve economies of scale. Small-scale units of technology can provide more flexibility by enabling capacity to be provided by a number of small units in different configurations rather than by just one large unit. These systems are also more robust against disruption than large-scale units are because output is spread over a number of units. The investment required for each additional small-scale unit is also smaller than that of larger units, with a faster payback period, encouraging investment in the latest technology.

## *Degree of automation of the technology*

The degree of automation refers to the extent to which the technology operates without human intervention. There is a continuum from low automation (high degree of human intervention – e.g. driving a car) to high automation (occasional intervention – e.g. monitoring a chemical plant), and the level of automation depends on the level of complexity and intuition required. The advantages of automation are that it permits repetitive tasks to be executed with precision, speed and power and can lower direct labour costs. The disadvantages of automation include the possible loss of flexibility and creativity due to the lack of human intervention and potential high support costs, such as the labour costs of support engineers.

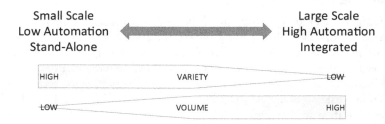

*Figure 6.1* The relationship between process technology and volume/variety

### *Degree of integrating of the technology*

The degree integrating the technology refers to the extent to which individual units of technology are connected together. Process technologies are increasingly connected together – for example, material processing systems such as FMC, FMS and CIM and information processing systems through the use of Internet-based systems. The advantages of integration are that it reduces fragmentation of previously separated processes and can lead to improved synchronization and thus reduced work in progress (WIP) and costs. The disadvantage of integration is high capital costs and the increased exposure to the risk of failure.

In making a choice regarding process technology in general, investments in large-scale, highly automated and integrated technology are appropriate for a high-volume/low-variety mix where the emphasis is on low cost rather than flexibility. Investments in small-scale, low-automation (people-based) and stand-alone technologies are appropriate for a low-volume/high-variety mix where the emphasis is on flexibility rather than low cost (Figure 6.1).

## Reference

Slack, N., Brandon-Jones, A., and Johnston, R. (2016) *Operations Management*, 8th edn., Pearson Education Limited.

# 7 Product and service design

The ability to quickly develop new products and services can provide a source of competitive advantage in offering something unique to the market that can then lead to increased market share and/or increased profitability. Innovations may come from either a technology-push approach aligned with a resource-based operations strategy or a market-pull approach associated with a market-based operations strategy. The product life cycle model puts the design process into a strategic context by highlighting how different phases over the life of a product or service can impact both the product design and also process design requirements. In general, the model predicts an emphasis on innovation and customization in product design in the early introductory phase of a product, giving way to standardization and an emphasis on efficient process design at the mature phase of the life cycle.

## The design process

The steps involved in the design process are now described.

### *Idea generation*

The source of new ideas for products and services can come from either seeking to exploit developments in technology or seeking to fulfil market demand primarily from suggestions from customers and competitors. Customers are an important source of information regarding new ideas in product and service development. Customer views can be collected using data-collection methods such as questionnaires and focus group interviews. Competitors can provide a good source of ideas, and it is important that the organization analyses any new products or services as they are introduced to the market and makes an appropriate response. Reverse engineering is a systematic approach to dismantling and inspecting a competitor's product to look for aspects of design that could be incorporated into the organization's own product. This is especially prevalent when the product is a complex assembly, such as a car, where design choices are myriad.

### Feasibility study

The marketing function will take the ideas created in the idea generation stage and form a series of alternative concepts on which a feasibility study is undertaken. The concept refers to the combination of physical products and services, referred to as the package, which delivers a set of expected benefits to the customer. Once a concept has been formulated, it must then be submitted to and pass three tests:

1   Market analysis: will it sell in sufficient numbers?
2   Economic analysis: can we make a profit on projected sales?
3   Technical analysis: have we the technical capability to introduce the concept to the market?

Note that the concept should pass all three tests. So although our concept may be popular with customers, unless we can make a profit on the projected sales volume, the concept is unlikely to be pursued. The market analysis should identify whether sufficient demand for the proposed product or service exists and assess its fit with the existing marketing strategy. To perform an economic analysis, an accurate estimate of demand is required on the basis of a predicted price range for the product or service, one that is compatible with its position in the market. Then estimates of costs on such factors as staffing, materials and equipment must be obtained. Techniques such as a cost–benefit analysis, decision theory and accounting measures (such as net present value (NPV) and internal rate of return (IRR)) may be used to calculate the profitability of a product. The technical analysis involves determining whether the technical capability to manufacture the product or deliver the service exists in the organisation proposing to introduce it. This covers such issues as ensuring materials are available to make the product to the specification required, ensuring the appropriate machinery and skills are available to work with these materials and securing the staff skills necessary to deliver a service.

### Preliminary design

The specification of the concept – what the product or service should do to satisfy customer needs – is translated into a technical specification of the components of the package (the product and service components that satisfy the customer needs defined in the concept) and the process by which the package is created. The specification of the components of the package requires a product and service structure that describes the relationship between the components and a bill of materials (BOM) or list of component quantities derived from the product structure.

## Final design

The final design stage involves refining the preliminary design by using a prototype until a viable final design can be made. The final design will be assessed according to three main facets: functional design, form design and production design.

### Functional design

Functional design entails ensuring that the design meets the performance characteristics that are specified in the product concept. Two aspects of functional design are reliability and maintainability. Reliability measures the probability that a product or service will perform its intended function for a specified period of time under normal conditions of use. Strategies for improving product or service reliability include simplified design (for example, fewer parts in a product), improving reliability in individual elements of the product or service and adopting backup product or service elements. Maintainability is the ability of the customer to maintain a product or the need for trained personnel to undertake maintenance or repair activities. Maintainability is connected to issues such as the cost of the product (it may be cheaper to throw away rather than to repair the product) and its reliability (high reliability will reduce the importance of maintainability). Maintainability can be improved by modular design to enable whole modules to be replaced rather than the lengthy investigation of faults. Maintenance schedules should also be specified to help prevent problems from occurring.

### Form design

Form design refers to product aesthetics such as look and feel. This is particularly important for consumer durables, but even industrial appliances should at least project an image of quality. In services, the design of the supporting facility, such as the room decor, lighting and music in a restaurant, provide an important element of the service design.

### Production design

Production design involves ensuring that the design takes into consideration the ease and cost of manufacture of a product. Good design will take into consideration the present manufacturing capabilities from material supplies, equipment and personnel skills available. The cost of production can be reduced by simplification (reducing the number of components, subassemblies and options in a product, thus reducing the amount of manufacturing processes required), standardization (enabling the use of the same components for different products and modules) and modularization (combining standardized building blocks in different ways to create a range of products).

### *Mass customisation*

Mass customization attempts to combine high-variety, high-volume output to provide the customer with customized products at a relatively low price. Therefore, mass customization aims to mass-produce a basic family of products or services that can still be customized to the needs of individual customers. One way of achieving mass customization is to incorporate the ideas related to production design of simplification, standardization and modularization. Vonderembse and White (2004) describe three levels of customization:

1   Customer-contact customization involves the product or service being tailored to individual needs. For example, a haircut or bicycle can be designed and delivered to meet the specification provided by an individual customer.
2   Adaptive customization involves a standard product or service that can be customized to meet individual needs. For example, a car can be customized by the customer by ordering from a list of options, such as metallic paint and air conditioning. Here customization starts at the production rather than design stage.
3   Presentation customization involves standard products being presented differently to different customers. This can be achieved through differences in elements such as packaging, delivery channel, terms and conditions of purchase and stated use. Here the level of customization occurs after the product has been produced.

## Service design

The design process outlined in the previous section of this chapter is relevant both to products and to services. This section outlines issues relevant to the design of services in particular. In addition, to the intangible nature of service design, the nature of the service can be affected by the presence of the customer in the service delivery process, and most services are accompanied by some sort of tangible element. This combination of elements is termed 'the service package' (Fitzsimmons and Fitzsimmons, 2011) and is defined as a bundle of goods and services with information that is provided in some environment. The service package consists of the following five features, using a hotel business as an example and laying out criteria of how each of these features could be evaluated as appropriate for the service package offered:

1   A supporting facility is the physical resources that must be in place before a service can be offered (e.g. hotel building). Criteria for evaluation include the location, interior decoration, supporting equipment, architectural appropriateness and facility layout.
2   Facilitating goods are the material purchased or consumed by the buyer or the items provided by the customer (e.g. towels, soap etc.). Criteria for evaluation include consistency, quantity and selection.
3   Information is the data that are available from the customer or provider to enable efficient and customized service (e.g. room reservation information). Criteria for evaluation include accuracy, timeliness and usefulness.
4   Explicit services are the benefits that are readily observable by the senses and consist of the essential or intrinsic features of the service (e.g. a comfortable bed in a clean room). Criteria for evaluation include personnel training, comprehensiveness, consistency and availability.
5   Implicit services are the psychological benefits that the customer may sense only vaguely or the extrinsic features of the service (e.g. friendly and helpful service at reception). Criteria for evaluation include attitude of service, atmosphere, waiting time, status, sense of well-being, privacy and security and convenience.

The idea of the service package shows that although service design is often primarily related to the design of the process of delivering the service, it can be seen that the service package also requires the design of physical aspects such as the supporting facility and facilitating goods. However, service design must take into account how the individual customer may react to the service as it is delivered. This is not easy to account for, because all customers are different and have different expectations of what the service should provide. This requires close cooperation between operations and marketing to identify a target customer market and ensure that the service design is meeting their needs.

### *3D printing*

Three-dimensional (3D) printing or additive manufacturing takes a computer-based 3D model and then builds a physical representation of that model by rendering it sequentially as a number of layers. The technique has its roots in prototyping but is now used in final design and for manufacturing final products. 3D printing produces objects by adding material rather than mechanically removing material from a solid block. The 3D-printing process involves making a product from sequential layers of fine powder or liquid by using materials such as metals, plastics and composite materials. 3D printing is especially attractive for producing low volumes of products and is gaining importance for producing prototypes and small production runs. Further advantages of 3D printing include its greater scope for complex designs, a more rapid market launch and waste reduction for a more efficient manufacturing process. Disadvantages include the high cost of high-volume output, the limited range of printable materials and limitations on the size of the components that can be printed.

## References

Fitzsimmons, J.A. and Fitzsimmons, M.J. (2011) *Service Management: Operations, Strategy, and Information Technology*, 7th edn., McGraw-Hill.

Vonderembse, M.A. and White, G.P. (2004) *Core Concepts of Operations Management*, John Wiley & Sons.

# 8 Process design

Although organisations are often structured around functional areas such as marketing and finance, the value that the customer obtains from a product or service, in terms of operations, is a result of a set of (transformation) processes. Thus, well-designed processes that meet the needs of the customer are essential if an organization is to be competitive. The design of processes may be determined by customer requirements or benchmarking competitors or may be directly related to meeting strategic objectives such as order-winning competitive factors. The design of processes is complex, so the steps in a structured approach to process design are covered as is the use of tools to assist process design activities such as process mapping, service blueprints and business process simulation. The task of designing processes should be undertaken as follows:

1    Identify opportunities for process improvement.
2    Document the process design.
3    Redesign the process.

## 1 Identify opportunities for process improvement

The main generic processes in an organization can be described as supplier relationship, new product development, order fulfilment and customer relationship. These represent the core processes involved in adding value to the organization's customers, thus providing a general guide to where improvement efforts should be focused. These processes will in most organizations be too large and complex to evaluate in a single initiative, and thus it is necessary to scope the project to address a particular area of concern. These areas can be derived from customer feedback, employee ideas generated from suggestion schemes and benchmarking against competitors.

## 2 Document the process design

Identifying activities in a current process design involves a data-collection exercise that uses methods such as an examination of current documentation, interviews and observation. To provide a framework for the design and improvement of service processes, the documentation techniques of process mapping and service blueprinting can be used.

### *Process mapping*

Documenting the process can be undertaken by constructing a process map, also called a flow chart. This is a useful way of understanding any business process and showing the interrelationships between activities in a process. This can help in identifying and fixing problems with the process, assisting the development of new processes and comparing the design of similar processes. For larger projects, it may be necessary to represent a given process at several levels of detail. Thus, a single activity may be shown as a series of sub-activities on a separate diagram. Figure 8.1 shows the representations used in a simple process-mapping diagram.

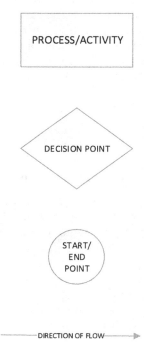

*Figure 8.1* Symbols used in a process map

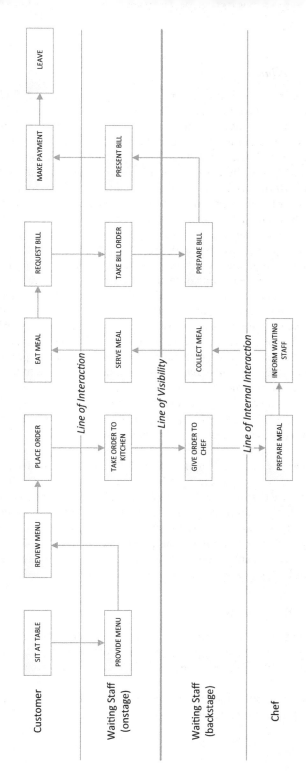

*Figure 8.2* Service blueprint for a restaurant

### Service blueprinting

Process maps are widely used in manufacturing to design the flow of a number of linked processes that produce an output. In services, however, process maps may be less relevant when a service consists of a number of sub-processes that are not linked and the service 'output' is a number of customer-employee interactions. In this case, the process design may first focus on the design of the customer-employee interactions and then identify external performance measures such as customer satisfaction. To assist in the analysis of customer-employee interactions, process maps can be extended to show how a business interacts with customers. A service blueprint is a flow chart that structures the process activities on either side of a customer *line of visibility*. The activities above the line are visible to the customer, and those below the line are operations that the customer does not see. Activities above the line of visibility are subdivided into two fields, separated by the *line of interaction*, which divides activities undertaken by the customer and the service provider. Below the line of visibility, a *line of internal interaction* separates the activities of front-line personnel who set up actions before providing a service (not in view of the customer) and support personnel who contribute materials or services required to provide the service. Finally, the *line of implementation* separates support activities from management activities such as planning, controlling and decision-making. Figure 8.2 shows an example of a service blueprint for a restaurant.

The objective of the service blueprint is that it not only charts the service process flow as does a process map but also shows the structure of the service organization on the vertical axis, showing relationships between, for example, internal customers, support staff and front-line providers. In particular, the diagram aims to highlight the interactions between the customer and process where customer services can be affected. The diagrams can also be used as a design tool to determine staffing levels, job descriptions and the selection of equipment and as a control tool to identify gaps in service provision by analysing fail points. Fail points are potential service system shortfalls between what the service delivers and what the targeted customers have been led to expect.

## 3   Redesign the process

There are many ways that a process can be redesigned to meet particular objectives, so it is necessary to generate a range of innovative solutions for evaluation. The following are three approaches to generating new ideas:

1   *Brainstorming* offers the greatest scope for radical improvements to the process design but represents a risk in the implementation of a totally

new approach. A deep understanding of the process is required so that the design will be feasible.

2   *Modifying existing designs* is less risky than a blue-skies approach but may mean that the opportunity for a radical improvement in process design is missed.

3   *Using an established 'benchmark' design* applies the idea of identifying the best-in-class performer for the particular process in question and adopting that design. Disadvantages to this approach may be that the process design of the best-in-class performer may not be available or the context of the best-in-class performer may not match the context for the new design.

The process map or service blueprint provides an overall view of the current or expected process design, and this should be used so that an overall view is taken when process design options are generated. This helps to ensure that design solutions proposed in a specific area do not have a detrimental effect in other areas of the process and thus affect overall process performance. The design of service processes in particular is a key factor in meeting the needs of the customer. In services, the process incorporates employees, customers and facilitating goods in a dynamic event that may be undertaken in a different manner each time, according to the demands of the individual customer. The interaction between the customer and service provider can be analysed using the service blueprint diagrams described in this chapter. It will be necessary to reduce the number of design alternatives generated, and this can be achieved by a rating scheme that scores each design solution against key performance dimensions, such as response time and cost of operation. The outcome of this analysis will be a reduced number of design solutions, which can then be subjected to more detailed analysis using tools such as business process simulation.

### *Business process simulation*

Business process simulation (BPS) allows the performance of the organization to be observed quickly and under a number of different scenarios. The simulation method refers to both the process of building a model and the conducting of experiments on that model. BPS is usually implemented by using discrete-event simulation systems that move through time in (discrete) steps (Greasley, 2019).

## Reference

Greasley, A. (2019) *Simulating Business Processes for Descriptive, Predictive and Prescriptive Analytics*, De Gruyter.

# 9　Job design

A key aspect of operations is the management of the organisation's human resources. Most people in an organisation will be involved in undertaking operations activities and the operations function should contribute to the human resource strategy of the company. There are many aspects to managing people in the organisation including the design of project structures covered in chapter 16. This chapter is focussed on the issue of job design as it relates to human resources. This is particularly relevant to services where it is likely that the customer may be involved in the actual delivery of the service. This means service employees and customers frequently work together, and thus the behaviour of employees is likely to have a major effect on the customer's perceived level of service quality. The implication is that employees that are not motivated will be dissatisfied and that this will lead to a poor perception of service quality by customers. Technology is often used as a way of 'controlling' employee behaviour in these circumstances, but in services, in particular, it is difficult to completely replace the element of human interaction.

## The job characteristics model

The Hackman and Oldham (1980) job characteristics model can provide suggestions on how to structure jobs to include more motivators. The model links job characteristics to the desired psychological state of the individual and outcomes in terms of motivation and job performance (Figure 9.1). The model takes into account individual differences and provides a structure for analysing motivational problems at work and to predict the effects of change on people's jobs and to help plan new work systems. The model proposes five desirable characteristics of a job:

1　Skill variety (SV) – the extent to which a job makes use of different skills and abilities.
2　Task identity (TI) – the extent to which a job involves completing a whole identifiable piece of work rather than simply a part.

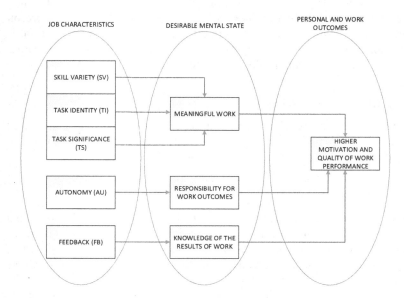

*Figure 9.1* The job characteristics model

3    Task significance (TS) – the extent to which a job affects other people, both inside and outside the organization.
4    Autonomy (AU) – the extent to which the job allows the job holder to exercise choice and discretion in their work.
5    Feedback (FB) – the extent to which the job itself (as opposed to other people) provides the job holder with information on their performance.

The model proposes that the presence of these characteristics will lead to desirable mental states in terms of meaningful work (SV, TI, TS), responsibility for outcomes of work (AU) and knowledge of the results of work (FB). These mental states will in turn lead to higher motivation and quality of work performance. The effects predicted by the model are moderated by factors such as the importance that an individual attaches to challenge and personal development.

The five core job characteristics can be combined to provide a motivating potential score (MPS) by using the following formula:

$$MPS = \left[ \frac{(SV + TI + TS)}{3} \right] \times AU \times FB$$

The formula shows that the addition of SV, TI and TS means that a low score on one of these variables can be compensated by a high score on another. The formula also shows that the combined effect of these three variables (which are divided by 3) is only equal to the other two job characteristics (autonomy and feedback) on their own.

## Job design approaches

The following are examples of approaches to job design that have been used in an attempt to bring these desirable job characteristics to people's work, to lead to an improved mental state and thus increased performance.

### *Job rotation*

Job rotation involves a worker changing job roles with another worker on a periodic basis. If successfully implemented this can help increase task identity, skill variety and autonomy through involvement in a wider range of work tasks, with discretion about when these mixes of tasks can be undertaken. However, this method does not actually improve the design of jobs and it can mean that people gravitate to jobs that suit them and are not interested in initiating rotation with colleagues. At worst it can mean rotation between various boring jobs with no acquisition of new skills.

### *Job enlargement*

Job enlargement involves the horizontal integration of tasks to expand the range of tasks involved in a particular job. If successfully implemented, this can increase task identity, task significance and skill variety by involving the worker in the whole work task either individually or in a group.

### *Job enrichment*

Job enrichment involves the vertical integration of tasks and the integration of responsibility and decision-making. If successfully implemented, this can increase all five of the desirable job characteristics by involving the worker in a wider range of tasks and providing responsibility for the successful execution of these tasks. This technique requires feedback so that the success of the work can be judged. The managerial and staff responsibilities potentially given to an employee through enrichment can be seen as a form of empowerment. This should in turn lead to improved productivity and product quality. Although job enrichment may affect supervisory levels of management, by replacing a supervisor with a team leader, for example, the power structure used to justify management decisions for personal objectives remains intact.

## Learning curves

Organizations have often used learning curves to predict the improvement in productivity that can occur as experience in a process is gained. Thus, learning curves can give an organization a method of measuring continuous improvement activities. If a firm can estimate the rate at which an operation time will decrease, then it can predict the impact on cost and increase in effective capacity over time. The learning curve is based on the concept that when productivity doubles, the decrease in time per unit is the rate of the learning curve. Thus, if the learning curve is at a rate of 85%, the second unit takes 85% of the time of the first unit, the fourth unit takes 85% of the second unit, the eighth unit takes 85% of the fourth and so on. Learning curves are usually applied to individual operators, but the concept can also be applied in a more aggregate sense, called an experience curve or improvement curve, and applied to such areas as manufacturing system performance or cost estimating. Industrial sectors can also be shown to have different rates of learning. However, improvements along a learning curve do not just happen, and the theory is most applicable to new product or process development, where scope for improvement is greatest or businesses that include complex repetitive operations where the work pace is determined mostly by people, not machines. Examples of industries that use learning curves include construction, defence, aerospace and electronics. The learning curve effect in simple routine processes such as mass production may show improvement only for a short time, so their use is more limited. Using learning curves comes with step changes that can slow or accelerate the rate of learning, such as organizational change, changes in technology or quality improvement programmes. Learning effects also take place as the result of action. To ensure learning occurs, the organization must invest in factors such as research and development, advanced technology, people and continuous improvement efforts.

## Reference

Hackman, J.R., and Oldham, G.R. (1980) *Work Redesign*, Prentice Hall.

# 10 Operations planning and control

Operations planning and control is about matching the capacity of the organization with customer demand. The two areas are now considered separately.

## Operations planning

Operations planning is concerned with taking actions, such as ensuring resources are in place, in anticipation of future events. The nature of the planning task is determined by how accurately future events can be predicted. The predictability of demand for goods and services can range from a situation of what is essentially dependent demand (demand can be predicted) to a high level of unpredictability (independent demand). In a dependent, demand-type situation, it is not necessary to activate a planning system and acquire resources until a delivery date for an order is received. Both transforming resources and transformed resources may be acquired at the appropriate time for delivery. This is called a resource-to-order planning policy and is associated with construction and project-based operations. In an independent demand situation, when demand is relatively predictable, the transforming resources, such as staff and machinery, may be in place on a permanent basis. However, the transformed resources – the raw material that is used to construct the product – may be acquired on the receipt of a customer's order. This is called a make-to-order planning policy. Despite the risk of stockouts (being out of stock), many manufacturers and retailers use this strategy because it decreases the amount of inventory through the supply chain. Finally, if demand is unpredictable, the organization will use a make-to-stock planning policy, which produces to a forecast of demand for the product. This approach may be used by retailers who need the products on display for people to buy.

Whereas the customer will 'see' only the delivery time from stock in a make-to-stock system, in a make-to-order system, the delivery cycle will

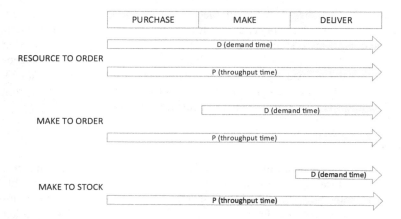

*Figure 10.1* Planning policies for demand types

include the purchase, make and delivery stages. This effect is examined by using P:D ratios. The P:D ratio compares the demand time D (from customer request to receipt of goods/services) to the total throughput time P of the purchase, make and delivery stages. The purchase stage involves acquiring the necessary resources from internal and external suppliers; the make stage includes the processing of resources through the operations system; and the deliver stage involves packing and distributing the finished good to the customer. The relationship between the planning and control systems and the P:D ratio is shown in Figure 10.1.

The P:D ratio makes the implications for the delivery time to the customer explicit. In a *resource-to-order* system, the purchase, make and deliver stages all affect delivery performance. In a *make-to-order* system transforming resources are in place but the customer has to wait for the product to be made and delivered. In a make-to-stock system, however, the customer 'sees' only the delivery time. Although delivery performance is improved in a *make-to-stock system*, the item is being produced to a forecast demand, which is subject to error.

## Operations control

Although operations planning will attempt to anticipate events, there may be a mismatch between current actions and what is actually required due to unforeseen events or behaviours. An example would be an unforeseen change in customer demand for the mix of goods and services offered. Operations control is concerned with ensuring that the current behaviour of the operations system conforms to the required behaviour. This section examines the activities associated with operations control tasks. These generally consist of loading (determining the current capacity and volumes), sequencing (deciding on the order of execution of work) and scheduling (allocating start and finish times for a customer order).

## *Loading*

Loading involves determining the available capacity for each stage in a process and allocating a work task to that stage. The calculation of available capacity must take account of both planned factors such as machine maintenance and unplanned factors such as machine breakdowns and worker absenteeism. These issues are dealt with in more detail in Chapter 11. There are two principal approaches to loading: finite and infinite. Finite loading allocates work up to an agreed fixed (finite) upper limit. This may be because the upper limit of capacity is fixed, such as that for aircraft seats. The upper limit can be fixed through a policy, such as using an appointment system. Finally, there may be a policy of limiting the availability of the product or service to the market, such as a limited edition of an expensive watch may enhance demand. Infinite loading does not place a limit on the work loaded onto a stage. This may be because it is not possible to limit demand. For example, emergency hospital treatment should not be refused. In manufacturing or services, if demand exceeds capacity, a queue will form. This may be acceptable in some instances, such as shopping outlets, when the customer understands the cost of always providing instant service is too high.

## *Sequencing*

Sequencing (also known as dispatching) is the sequential assignment of tasks or jobs to individual processes. To attempt to control the progress of a job through a process, a job priority system is used. The priority of jobs queuing at a process determines the order in which they are processed. The difficulty lies in determining an appropriate priority rule to obtain the best performance. Priority rules include the following:

- DD (due date) – job with the nearest customer delivery due date to the current date.
- FCFS (first come, first served) – job arriving first at a process.

- SPT (shortest process time) – job with shortest process time.
- LPT (longest process time) – job with longest process time.

All the rules have different advantages and disadvantages. The DD rule tends to minimize the lateness of individual jobs, but it may lead to other jobs being delayed. The FCFS rule is easy to apply and is used for ease when no particular sequencing activities are necessary when the workload on the system is low. The SPT rule ensures that jobs with the shortest process time progress rapidly; thus, the number of jobs processed should be high. This rule will generally give the best performance in a congested system. However, a disadvantage of the SPT rule is that when the demand on the process is high, this may mean a job with a relatively long process time may have an unacceptably long wait and is always at the end of the queue. The LPT rule may be used when larger jobs can be completed in-house and smaller jobs can be subcontracted when their due date is near.

Rules can also use a combination of factors to determine the sequence, such as the critical ratio (CR), which is the ratio of the time left until the job's due date to the expected elapsed time for the job to be processed through the remaining processes to its completion. If the ratio is less than 1, the job is behind schedule and should receive priority.

$$\text{Critical ratio (CR)} = (\text{due date} - \text{current date}) \div \text{days required to complete job}$$

### *Scheduling*

Scheduling is the allocation of a start time and a finish time to each order while taking into account the loading and sequencing policies employed. The scheduling process is usually driven by the need to manage a number of jobs or customers in the system and ensure they are completed or receive their order by a target due date. This often necessitates rescheduling orders, called expediting, in order to ensure targets are actually met. In theory, expediting should not be necessary if planning and control activities have been undertaken correctly. However, in reality, due to the complexity of the task and unexpected events (for example, poor quality material in the process that leads to rework or machine breakdown events), expediting on a day-to-day basis may be needed.

## Optimized production technology

Optimized production technology (OPT) is an operations control system that is based on the identification of bottlenecks in the production process. A bottleneck is a resource whose capacity is less than or equal to the demand placed on it. This approach attempts to avoid much of the complexity of scheduling, by focusing on bottlenecks. The idea is that system output is determined by bottlenecks so it is essential to schedule non-bottleneck resources to ensure maximum use of the bottleneck resources themselves.

# 11 Capacity management

In this chapter, medium-term capacity issues are considered. These are concerned mainly with ensuring that sufficient capacity of the right type is available at the right time, to meet demand for the planning period. Setting capacity to meet the demands of the organization is termed 'capacity planning and control'. The capacity planning and control activity should measure demand, measure capacity and reconcile capacity and demand.

## Measuring demand

What makes demand particularly difficult to measure is the fact that it fluctuates in response to a number of influences. These include competitors introducing products or services into the marketplace that perform better on performance objectives such as higher quality, lower price or shorter delivery times. Also, changes in consumer tastes can affect demand as can changes to the economy, such as a recession.

The medium term is considered to be approximately 2 to 18 months, depending on the pace of change in the industry in which the organisation is competing. The planning process can be described as working in cycles, each cycle confirming detailed plans for the next time period and sketching more tentative plans for the following period. At the next planning meeting, these tentative plans are considered in more detail, and the cycle repeats. This process means that the organization can build on previous plans instead of attempting to devise new plans at each planning cycle. This reduces planning time and leads to more continuity in decision-making.

## Measuring capacity

Measuring capacity may seem straightforward at first, especially when compared to the uncertainty inherent in estimating demand. However, capacity is not fixed but is a variable that depends on a number of factors:

- Capacity takes many different forms, such as storage space, availability of employee skills, equipment numbers and transportation facilities.
- Any of these types of capacity may be the limiting factor or bottleneck on the capacity of a process. The actual bottleneck, and thus capacity, may also change over time.
- Working practices such as hours worked and holiday entitlement can also affect capacity calculations and may change over time. For example, a change in company policy may decrease the hours a week that employees can work and thus reduce capacity.
- The amount of capacity required to deliver a particular process at a particular level may change over time, due to the experience gained and improvements made to process design.
- The capacity available in multiple locations may not be simply summed as transportation time, and costs may make available capacity in a particular location unsuitable.
- Capacity is based on time, so underused capacity due to a drop in demand cannot be used later, when demand increases. Thus, the actual capacity available will be less the more that demand fluctuates. Process time fluctuations will also affect capacity.

Measuring capacity in services is a particular challenge. Generally, services need to be more custom-designed and involve more personal contact to meet specific customer needs. Customer involvement tends to provide an opportunity for special requests and instructions to be issued by the customer, and they tend to disrupt routine procedures and thus efficiency. Capacity may be lost in providing conversation to the customer in addition to delivering the actual service. Quality is closely related to the customer's perception of satisfactory service. Operations employees employed where high levels of customer contact occur must be skilled in interpreting what the customer really wants. Thus, the level of customer-client contact can have a direct effect on the efficiency and thus capacity availability that an operation can achieve. Two further issues to consider when measuring capacity are product mix and the definitions of design and effective capacity.

### *Product mix*

Only when a narrow product (or service) range is involved can capacity be measured reasonably accurately and in this case be quoted in terms of output volume. With a changing product mix, therefore, it may be more useful to measure capacity in terms of input measures, which provide some indication of the potential output. Also, for planning purposes, when demand is stated in output terms, input measures need to be converted to an estimated output measure. For example, in hospitals that undertake a range of activities, capacity is often measured in terms of beds available, an input measure. An output measure, such as number of patients treated per week, highly depends on the mix of activities that the hospital performs. Estimates of capacity based on output can also be misleading because part of this output may be accounted for by either inventory (for example, patients) part way through the process or the use of additional resources (for example, overtime, equipment rental, contracting out) that could not normally be treated as part of the organization's capacity.

### *Design, effective and actual capacity*

The *design capacity* of an operation represents the theoretical output of a process as it was designed. However, this level of capacity is rarely met, due to occurrences that prevent the operation producing its full output. These occurrences are called planned factors and unplanned factors. Planned factors are activities whose timing can be determined in advance. They include such items as maintenance, training and machine setup time. During these activities, the output from the operation is lost. In services, training personnel may take place during the part of the year when seasonal demand is low.

The capacity remaining after a loss of output due to planned factors is called the *effective capacity* of the process. However, this will also be above the level of capacity that is available due to unplanned occurrences such as machine breakdowns and worker absenteeism. These are more difficult to deal with than planned factors are, because by definition, their timing cannot be predicted. To minimize these disturbances, action such as preventive maintenance should be taken. This involves undertaking planned maintenance activities, if possible, when demand is low. These activities can include replacing equipment parts before they fail, to reduce unplanned breakdowns. Worker absenteeism could be reduced by improving motivation.

After taking both planned and unplanned factors into account, there remains the capacity available for processing, called the *actual capacity* of the operation.

## Reconciling capacity and demand

Methods for reconciling capacity and demand can be classified into three 'pure' strategies: level capacity, chase demand and demand management.

Due to the complexity of capacity management and the need to optimize a range of performance objectives, it is usually necessary to combine the three pure strategies described and form a mixed capacity-planning strategy.

### *Level capacity*

The level capacity strategy sets the processing capacity at a uniform level throughout the planning period, regardless of fluctuations in forecast demand. This means output is set at a fixed rate, usually to meet average demand. Inventory is used to absorb variations in demand. During periods of low demand, any overproduction can be transferred to finished goods inventory in anticipation of sales at a later time period (Figure 11.1). The disadvantage of this strategy is the cost of holding inventory and the cost of perishable items that may have to be discarded. To avoid producing obsolete items, firms try to create inventory for products that are relatively certain to be sold. This strategy is also of limited value for perishable goods.

For a service organization, output cannot be stored as inventory, so a level capacity plan involves running at a uniformly high level of capacity (Figure 11.2). The drawback of the approach is the cost of maintaining this high level of capacity, although it could be useful when the cost of lost sales is particularly high. To overcome this problem, the concept of partitioning demand is used, which involves keeping capacity in the customer-contact area consistently high, so that customers are not kept waiting, and keeping capacity in the noncontact areas at a more uniform level. Another strategy is for services to 'store' their output by performing part of their work in anticipation of demand. An example is purchasing and displaying goods before actual customer demand occurs.

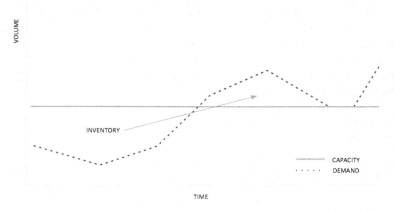

*Figure 11.1* Level capacity plan in manufacturing

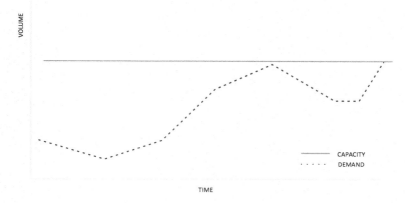

*Figure 11.2* Level capacity plan in services

### Chase demand

The chase demand strategy seeks to match output to the demand pattern over time. Capacity is altered by such policies as changing the amount of part-time staff, changing the amount of staff availability through overtime work, changing equipment levels and subcontracting. The strategy is costly in terms of activities such as overtime payments and changing staffing levels. The costs may be particularly high in industries in which skills are scarce. Disadvantages of subcontracting include a reduced profit margin lost to the subcontractor, loss of control, potentially longer lead times and the risk that the subcontractor may decide to enter the same market. For these reasons, a pure chase demand strategy is more usually adopted by service operations that cannot store their output and so make a level capacity plan less attractive. A graphical representation of a chase demand plan is shown in Figure 11.3.

In services, when the operation cannot usually match the demand rate with its capacity level, its objective becomes one of developing a capacity profile that matches its demand profile to the extent that this is feasible and economically viable. The following are some of the strategies for achieving this:

- Staggered work-shift schedules: scheduling the availability of capacity to cover demand involves constructing work shifts so that the number of operators available at any one time matches the demand profile – for example, in a fast-food restaurant.

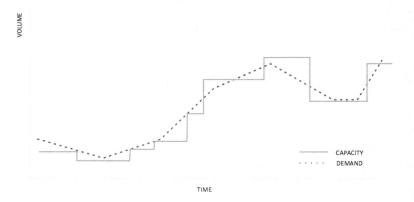

*Figure 11.3* Chase demand plan

- Part-time staff: more flexibility to schedule and smooth the work demand is often available for those parts of a service where the customer is not present and the service is provided by working with some surrogate for the customer. A strategy of using part-time staff needs to trade off the cost of not doing some work against the extra cost of employing the staff.
- Subcontractors: if there is not enough capacity, additional capacity can be obtained from outside sources – for example, surgeries employing contract doctor services to cover weekends.
- Multi-skilled floating staff: having multi-skilled staff increases flexibility in capacity decisions. For example, in the case of a hospital, it might be desirable to have some floating capacity that can be shifted from one department to another if the number of patients or the amount of nursing attention required in each department varies.
- Customer self-service: with this option, the service capacity arrives when the demand does. Customers at supermarkets and many department stores select most of their own merchandise.

### *Demand management*

While the level capacity and chase demand strategies aim to adjust capacity to match demand, the demand management strategy attempts to adjust demand to meet available capacity. There are many ways this can be done, but most involve altering the marketing mix (for example, price or promotion) and require coordination with the marketing function. A graphical representation of a demand management plan is shown in Figure 11.4.

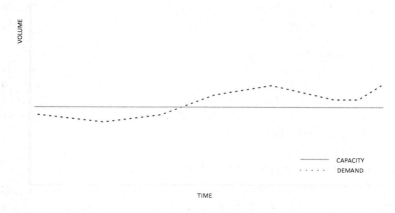

*Figure 11.4* Demand management plan

The following are some of the demand management strategies:

• Varying the price: during periods of low demand price discounts can be used to stimulate the demand level; conversely, when demand is higher than the capacity limit, price could be increased.
• Advertising: advertising and other marketing activities can be used to increase sales during low demand periods.
• Offering alternative products: this involves using existing processes to make or sell alternative products during low demand periods. An example is the way many garden centres use their premises to sell Christmas decorations during the winter months when gardening activity is low.
• Maintaining a fixed schedule: some services can schedule the times during which the service is available, such as airlines and rail services. Demand occurs as people purchase tickets to use some of the previously scheduled transportation capacity.
• Using an appointment system: the pattern of demand variations over the longer term can also have a significant influence on the planning of efficient service operations. The ideal would be to achieve uniform use of service capacity, but this is unlikely unless an appointment-only policy is in operation. Some services are provided by appointment, such as a dentistry or veterinary surgery. Using an appointment system permits demand to be moved into available time. The delay between a request for an appointment and the time of the appointment may depend on the backlog or queue of waiting work.

- Delaying delivery: delaying jobs until capacity is available serves to make the workload more uniform, such as the work of a bank teller. In addition, routine work may be set aside to make capacity available for rush jobs.
- Providing economic incentives for off-peak demand: some operations have a high capital investment in the capacity that they have to provide their services. Thus the unit cost of capacity that is used at peak demand periods is high. These operations try to keep demand as uniform as possible by using economic inducements such as off-peak electricity and off-peak telephone calls.

## Evaluating alternatives and making a choice

Capacity planning involves evaluating the capacity requirements and determining the best way to meet these by using a feasible and low-cost capacity-planning approach. The term 'aggregate planning' is sometimes used to describe the process of aggregating (grouping) capacity requirements over a medium-term planning horizon to provide the best way to meet these requirements. To choose a capacity plan that meets the aforementioned criteria, it is necessary to try to predict the consequences of that plan. One way of doing this that is particularly relevant to service operations is queuing theory.

### Queuing theory

In service situations, the output of the operation cannot be stored. Waiting time can be eliminated when customers are asked to arrive at fixed intervals (an appointment system) and when service times are fixed. Thus, waiting time in queues are caused by fluctuations in arrival rates and variability in service times. Queuing theory can be used to explore the trade-off between the amount of capacity and the customer arrival rate. Too much capacity and costs will be excessive, but too little capacity will cause a long wait for the customer and reduce service quality, leading to a loss of business. In a service context, queuing theory can provide a useful guide in determining an expected waiting time for an arriving customer and the average number of customers who will be waiting for service. This permits an estimate of the amount of capacity that will be needed to keep waiting time to a reasonable level, taking into account the expected rate and variability of demand. Examples of queuing situations include customers at a bank, aeroplanes circling and waiting to land, patients waiting to see a doctor and parts waiting to be processed at a machining centre. Uncertainty in arrival and service times means that even although on average there may be adequate capacity to meet demand, queuing may still occur when a number of successive arrivals or long service times occur. Conversely, idle time will occur when arrival rates or service time decreases. Although this behaviour means that full utilization will not be feasible for this type of system, queuing theory does allow for an analysis of how much capacity is needed to keep average or maximum queue length or waiting times to an acceptable level. This acceptable level, or service-quality level, depends on the type of operation involved.

Queue systems can be classified into a single-channel queuing system consisting of a single queue of customers who wait until a service facility is available and a multiple-channel queuing system that have parallel server facilities. Although a single queue system is increasingly popular and may be seen by customers as fairer in that it enforces the FCFS rule, its operation may not always be practical: imagine a single line of customers with trolleys/carts in a supermarket. Other disadvantages of a single queue system are that the length of the single queue may seem to imply a longer wait for customers than many short queues, and a single-channel queue system assumes that all the servers can meet the needs of all the customers.

## Forecasting demand

Accurate forecasts are an important factor in enabling organizations to deliver goods and services to the customer when required and thus achieve a quality service. Forecasting is important in relation to anticipating changing customer requirements and meeting them with new product and service designs. To produce accurate forecasts, an organization must collect up-to-date data on relevant information such as prices and sales volumes and choose an appropriate forecasting technique. The accuracy of a forecast also depends on the time horizon over which the forecast is derived. Forecasts for short time horizons tend to be more accurate than those for longer-term forecasts, so one way of improving accuracy is to shorten the lead time necessary for the organization to respond to a forecast. This might mean improving operations in terms of the flexibility performance objective. Organizations must develop forecasts on the level of demand that they should be prepared to meet. The forecast provides a basis for coordinating plans for activities in various parts of the organization, such as employing the right amount of personnel, purchasing the right amount of material and financing, which can help estimate the capital required for the business. Forecasts can be developed through either a qualitative approach or a quantitative approach. Qualitative forecasting methods take a subjective approach, are based on estimates and opinions and include techniques such as market surveys, the Delphi method and expert judgement. Quantitative forecasting methods use a mathematical expression or model to show the relationship between demand and some independent variable or variables. The model that is appropriate for forecasting depends on the demand pattern to be projected and the forecaster's objectives for the model. Quantitative forecasting techniques include time series analysis, moving averages, exponential smoothing, time series decomposition, and causal models such as regression analysis.

# 12 Inventory management

Inventory is present in all service and manufacturing processes. In manufacturing, inventory consists of the components that make up the product being manufactured. In services, inventory may be used as part of the service delivery system (for example, disposable implements for a hospital operation), or it may be part of the tangible component of the service itself (for example, the brochure for a car insurance policy). Inventory is important because although it is necessary for customer service it can also be a major cost to the organization. Although inventory management is often seen as an operational issue, it is important at a strategic level in that it may account for a far larger proportion of expenditure than may be allocated to other areas, such as labour costs. Furthermore, in strategic terms, inventory is now seen as a tool in meeting operations performance objectives such as cost, in addition to its role in lean operations in meeting speed and flexibility objectives.

## Types of inventory

All organizations will carry some inventory or stock of goods at any one time. This can range from items such as stationery to machinery parts or raw materials. Inventory can be classified by its position in the transformation process as inputs in the form of raw materials, within the transformation process termed 'WIP' or as outputs to the transformation process as finished goods. *Raw materials inventory* may be supplied in batches to secure quantity discounts and reduce material handling. However, smaller and more frequent order quantities translate into less inventory and may be achieved by negotiating smaller batches from suppliers. Variability in supplier lead times may be reduced by specifying longer but more reliable lead times from suppliers. *WIP inventory* may help uncouple production stages and provide greater flexibility in production scheduling. It can be minimized by eliminating obsolete stock, improving the operation's processes and reducing the number of products or services. *Finished goods inventory* may be used to ensure that important inventory items are always available to the customer or to avoid disruption caused by changing production output levels. It can be minimized by improving forecasts of customer demand and reducing fluctuations in demand caused by factors such as meeting end-of-period sales targets.

Inventory can also be considered in terms of its role in the operations process. For example, buffer or safety stock is used to compensate for the uncertainties inherent in the timing or rate of supply and demand between two operational stages and to compensate for uncertainties in supply between operational stages in a process due to factors such as equipment break-downs. Cycle inventory occurs when producing multiple products from one process in batches, because there is a need to produce enough to keep a supply while the other batches are being produced. Decoupling inventory is used to separate the operation of different stages in a process. It enables processes to run at their own speed and not match the rate of processing of different stages in the process. Anticipation inventory involves producing to stock to anticipate a predicted increase in demand. It may also be found as a consequence of policies such as buying in bulk to take advantage of price discounts. Finally, pipeline or movement inventory compensates for the lack of stock while material is being transported between processes. For example, the time delay in transportation from a warehouse to a retail outlet.

## Inventory models

Inventory models are analytical equations that are used to assess when inventory requires ordering and what quantity should be ordered at that point in time. In a *fixed order quantity* inventory system, inventory is ordered in response to some event, such as inventory falling to a particular level. The timing of the inventory order can be calculated using a reorder point (ROP) model. The quantity to order at this point in time may be calculated by using the economic order quantity (EOQ) model. In a *fixed order period* inventory system, inventory is ordered at a fixed point in time. A fixed order inventory (FOI) model can be used to determine the quantity to order at this point in time.

### The reorder point model

The reorder point (ROP) model identifies the time to order when the stock level drops to a predetermined amount. This amount will usually include a quantity of stock to cover for the delay between order and delivery (the delivery lead time) and an element of stock to reduce the risk of running out of stock when levels are low (the safety stock). To consider the probability of a stockout (an out-of-stock scenario), the idea of a service level is used, which is a measure of how sure the organization is that it can supply inventory from stock. This can be expressed as the probability that the inventory on hand during the lead time is sufficient to meet expected demand; for example, a service level of 90% means that there is a 0.90 probability that demand will be met during the lead time period and the probability that a stockout will occur is 10%. The reorder problem is one of determining the level of safety stock that balances the expected holding costs with the costs of stockout.

### The economic order quantity model

The EOQ model calculates the fixed inventory order volume required while seeking to minimize the sum of the annual costs of holding inventory and the annual costs of ordering inventory. The model makes a number of assumptions, including that demand is stable or constant; that ordering costs are fixed and identifiable; that the relationship between the cost of holding inventory and number of items held is linear; that the item cost does not vary with the order size; and that delivery lead times do not vary.

### The fixed order interval inventory model

The FOI model can be used to calculate the amount to order given a fixed interval between ordering. The calculation for the FOI model depends on whether demand and delivery lead times are treated as fixed or variable. A variation on the fixed order inventory system is when minimum and maximum levels are set for the inventory.

## Managing inventory – the ABC inventory classification system

One way of deciding the importance of inventory items and thus an appropriate inventory management method for them is to use the ABC classification system. Depending on the classification of the inventory, a fixed order quantity or fixed order period inventory system can be chosen to manage that system.

The ABC classification system sorts inventory items into groups according to the amount of annual expenditure they incur, which depends on the estimated number of items used annually multiplied by the unit cost. To instigate an ABC system, a table is produced that lists the items in expenditure order (with largest expenditure at the top) and shows the percentage of total expenditure and cumulative percentage of the total expenditure for each item.

By reading the cumulative percentage figure, it is usually found, following Pareto's law, that 10% to 20% of the items account for 60% to 80% of annual expenditure. These items are called A items and need to be controlled closely to reduce overall expenditure. Forecasting techniques may be used to improve the accuracy of demand forecasts for these items. Managing these items may also require a more strategic approach, which may translate into closer buyer-supplier relationships. A items may be managed by using a fixed order quantity system with perpetual inventory checks or a fixed order period system that uses a small time interval between review periods. The B items account for the next 20% to 30% of items and usually account for a similar percentage of total expenditure. These items require fewer inventory-level reviews than A items do. A fixed order period system with a minimum order level or a fixed order quantity system may be appropriate. Finally, C items represent the remaining 50% to 70% of items but only account for less than 25% of total expenditure. Here a fixed order quantity system may be appropriate, or less rigorous inventory control methods can be used, since the cost of inventory tracking will outweigh the cost of holding additional stock.

Overall expenditure may not be the only appropriate basis on which to classify items. Other factors include the importance of a component part on the overall product, the variability in delivery time, the loss of value through deterioration and the disruption caused to the production process if a stockout occurs.

# 13  Lean operations

Lean operations is defined in this chapter at one level as a philosophy and at another level as a collection of techniques, and its strategic significance can be considered at both of these levels. Implementing lean techniques can lead to improvements in cost and quality by reducing variability and waste. If lean is adopted as a philosophy, then it could provide a sustained competitive advantage and be considered part of a resource-based operations strategy. This is because adopting lean as a philosophy that permeates the organization, through the engagement of the workforce in continuous improvement techniques, for example, represents a much more difficult aim to achieve and so in turn creates a capability that is difficult to copy.

## The philosophy of lean operations

Two key issues at the core of the lean philosophy are to eliminate waste and to implement a continuous improvement programme.

### *Eliminate waste*

Waste is considered in the widest sense as any activity that does not add value to the operation. Bicheno (2004) states that although waste is strongly linked to lean, waste elimination is a means to achieving the lean ideal; it is not an end in itself; and waste prevention is at least as important as waste elimination.

Customer service wastes generally can be categorized as follows (Bicheno, 2004):

- Delay: customers waiting for service, for delivery, in queues, for response, not arriving as promised.
- Duplication: having to re-enter data, repeat details on forms and answering queries from several sources within the same organization.

- Unnecessary movements: queuing several times, poor ergonomics in the service encounter.
- Unclear communication: the waste of seeking clarification.
- Incorrect inventory: out-of-stock, unable to get exactly what is required, substitute products or services.
- Relationship failures: opportunities lost to retain or win customers, failure to establish rapport, ignoring customers, unfriendliness and rudeness.
- Mistakes: errors in the service transaction, product defects in the product-service bundle, lost or damaged goods.

In a manufacturing context, the seven types of waste identified by Ohno (1988) are as follows:

1  *Overproduction* is classified as the greatest source of waste and is an outcome of producing more than is needed by the next process.
2  *Waiting time* is the time spent by labour or equipment waiting to add value to a product. This may be disguised by undertaking unnecessary operations – for example, generating WIP on a machine – which are not immediately needed (the waste is converted from time to WIP).
3  *Unnecessarily transporting* WIP is another source of waste. Layout changes can substantially reduce transportation time.
4  *Unnecessary processes and operations* do not add value to the product but are simply there because of poor design or machine maintenance. Improved design or preventive maintenance should eliminate these processes.
5  *Inventory* of all types is considered as waste and should be eliminated.
6  *Complex work movement* is wasteful and should be simplified to reduce waste caused by unnecessary motion of labour and equipment.
7  *Defective goods* incur costs. The total costs of poor quality can be high and include scrap material, wasted labour time, time expediting orders and a loss of goodwill through missed delivery dates.

The root cause of much waste is variability and too-high utilization, which is expressed in Toyota's 3Ms of mura (variability), muri (utilization) and muda (waste) (Figure 13.1).

What the 3Ms' relationship shows is that mura (variability) leads to muri (higher utilization), which leads to muda (waste), which leads to mura, and the cycle is repeated. This implies that mura or variability is the root problem of waste in systems. For example, variability in demand causes stress in staff at peak times, leading to mistakes, which leads to higher utilization and deadlines being missed. However, muda can result in mura, due to lead times being long and quality being uncertain.

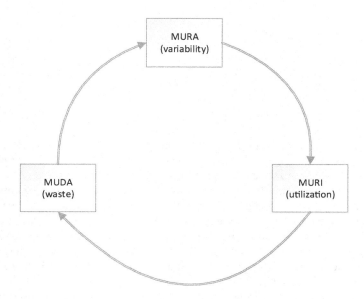

*Figure 13.1* Mura, muri and muda

Techniques to smooth flow and thus decrease variability include levelled scheduling and pull production systems, covered later in this chapter.

### Continuous improvement

Continuous improvement, or kaizen (the Japanese term), is a philosophy stating that it is possible to get to the ideals of lean by a continuous stream of improvements over time. Lean aims to create a new culture in which all employees are encouraged to contribute to continuous improvement efforts by generating ideas for improvements and perform a range of functions.

## Lean techniques

From the variety of lean techniques available, the use of pull production systems and levelled scheduling are considered here.

### Push production and pull production systems

In a push production system, a schedule pushes work on to machines, work that is then passed through to the next work centre (Figure 13.2).

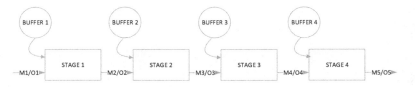

*Figure 13.2* Push production system

In Figure 13.2 materials (M1) and orders for production (O1) are pushed on to production stage 1. Production stage 1 then produces material for production stage 2, and the cycle repeats through the production stages. At each production stage, a buffer stock (buffer 1, buffer 2, etc.) is kept to ensure that if any production stage fails, then the subsequent production stage will not be starved of material. For example, if there is a breakdown at stage 2 of the production line, stage 3 will be fed from a buffer stock (buffer 3) until the problem has been fixed. The higher the buffer stocks kept at each stage of the line, the more disruption can occur without the production line being halted by lack of material.

Pull systems are sometimes called lean synchronization, meaning the customer gets what they want only when they want it, with minimal waste. In a pull system (Figure 13.3), the process is triggered by an order for the finished product at the end of the production line (O1). This then triggers an order for components of that item (O2), which in turn triggers an order for further subcomponents (O3). The process repeats until the initial stage of production and the material flows through the system as in the push approach. Using the pull system, the production system produces output at each stage only in response to demand and eliminates the need for buffer stock.

The aim of eliminating buffers between the production stages is to ensure a responsive system. However, the pull system does not overcome the basic characteristic of a line layout, namely that if one stage fails, then all subsequent stages will be starved of work and, in effect, output from the whole production line will be lost. This would seem to be a powerful argument for retaining buffers, but the JIT approach actually argues that the disruption that occurs due to the lack of buffer stock will motivate people to find the root cause of problems. Over time, this will lead to a more reliable and efficient system. Motivation will be generated by the highly visible nature of any problem occurring (it will bring the whole factory to a halt) and by the fact that the problem is now everyone's problem and not just a local difficulty of which no one else is aware. In moving from a push system to a pull system, it is common practice to gradually reduce the buffer levels as

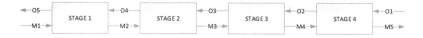

*Figure 13.3* Pull production system

the production system reliability is increased. Any attempt to move directly to eliminate buffers is likely to cause severe disruption to a system formerly reliant on this safety net.

The pull approach can also be applied to the relationship between customers and suppliers in the supply chain. Thus, suppliers in a lean supply chain are required to supply customers only in response to demand, and the customer will not keep buffer stocks just in case the supplier fails to deliver on time. This reduces inventory and increases responsiveness in the supply chain but does require close cooperation between customer and supplier and reliability in the supplier operations.

### Kanban production system

One system for implementing a pull system is called a kanban production system (kanban is Japanese for 'card' or 'sign'). Each kanban provides information on the part identification, quantity per container that the part is transported in and the preceding and next work stations. Kanbans, in themselves, do not provide the schedule for production, but without them, production cannot take place, because they authorize the production and movement of material through the pull system. Kanbans need not be a card but should be something that can be used as a signal for production, such as a marker or coloured square area. There are two types of kanban systems: the single-card and two-card.

The single-card system uses only one type of kanban card, called the conveyance kanban, which authorizes the movement of parts. The number of containers at a work centre is limited by the number of kanbans. A signal to replace inventory at the work centre can be sent only once the container has been emptied. Toyota use a dual card system that, in addition to the conveyance kanban, uses a production kanban to authorize the production of parts. This system permits greater control over production and inventory. If the processes are tightly linked (one always follows the other), then a single kanban can be used.

The system is implemented with a given number of cards in order to establish a smooth flow. The number of cards is then decreased, in turn decreasing inventory, and any problems that surface are tackled. Cards are decreased, one at a time, to continue the continuous improvement process. Importantly, successfully implementing a kanban system requires that a stable and reliable production system be in place.

### Heijunka *(levelled scheduling)*

The approach to scheduling which has been followed in traditional manufacturing systems is to make a large number of one product before switching to another. Unfortunately, this approach will lead to high levels of finished goods in inventory at certain times (for example the end of a production run), with the possibility of not being able to satisfy customer demand at other times (for example when long production runs of other goods are being manufactured). This approach also causes variability in work processes that can lead to waste. *Heijunka*, which means 'level production', attempts to overcome this problem by dividing the day into equal parcels of time and dividing up the work to fit into the parcels, thus creating a smooth flow of materials and components throughout the day. The flow is controlled by cards or other devices that authorize work to commence at the start of each time parcel, called pitch increments.

Using a traditional approach, a day's work of say 30 A products, 30 B products and 30 C products would be produced one after another – 30 A then 30 B then 30 C to minimize changeover costs. A level schedule might be AAABBBCCC repeated 10 times to smooth the flow. It is, however, usual when implementing *Heijunka* to use mixed-model scheduling and continually alternate between products giving ABCABCABC repeated 10 times. This creates a more even flow, and if a fault is found with any product type, then at least relatively few have been made. When a level assembly schedule has been achieved, the production of each item will closely match demand. However, because the flow of component parts must be adjusted to match the rate at which finished goods will be produced, it is necessary to match the cycle time (the rate of production) at the work centres with the demand rate.

## References

Bicheno, J. (2004) *The New Lean Toolbox: Towards Fast, Flexible Flow*, Picsie Books, Buckingham.

Ohno, T. (1988) *Toyota Production System: Beyond Large-Scale Production*, Productivity Inc.

# 14 Enterprise resource planning

This chapter covers the use of information systems that provide assistance to operations when planning to use resources in the transformation process. The chapter covers enterprise resource planning (ERP), materials requirements planning (MRP) and manufacturing resource planning (MRP II) systems.

## Enterprise resource planning systems

Enterprise resource planning systems (often called enterprise systems) support the business processes of an organization across functional boundaries in that organization. They use Internet technology to integrate information in the business and with external stakeholders such as customers, suppliers and partners. The main elements of an ERP system are concerned with internal production, distribution and financial processes but may also include elements such as the following:

- Customer relationship management (CRM), which is concerned with marketing and sales processes.
- Supply chain management (SCM), which is concerned with the flow of materials, information and customers through the supply chain.
- Supplier relationship management (SRM), which is concerned with all activities involved in obtaining items from a supplier, which include procurement and inbound logistics such as transportation, goods-in and warehousing before the item is used.

Other elements may include product lifecycle management (PLM), financial management and human capital management.

## Materials requirements planning

MRP is an information system used to calculate the requirements for component materials needed to produce end items. These components have what is called dependent demand. A dependent demand item has a demand that is relatively predictable because it depends on other factors. For example, a fireplace mantel consists of two legs and one shelf. If daily demand for the mantel, derived from the production schedule, is 50 mantels, then a daily demand of 100 legs and 50 shelves can be predicted. Thus, a dependent demand item can be classified as having a demand that can be calculated as the quantity of the item needed to produce a scheduled quantity of an assembly that uses that item. MRP systems manage dependent demand items by calculating the quantity needed and the timing required (taking into account purchasing and manufacturing lead times) of each item. The components of an MRP system that use and process this information are shown in Figure 14.1, and each component of the MRP system is now described.

### Master production schedule

An ideal master production schedule (MPS) is one that most efficiently uses the organization's capacity while being able to meet customer due dates. The master schedule provides a plan for the quantity and timing of when orders are required. The MRP system uses this information and, taking into account delivery, production and supply lead times, indicates when materials are needed to achieve the master schedule. The MPS usually shows plans based on time buckets of, for example, a day or a week. The length of the time bucket will generally be longer (for instance a month) for planning purposes and become shorter closer to the present time for detailed production planning tasks.

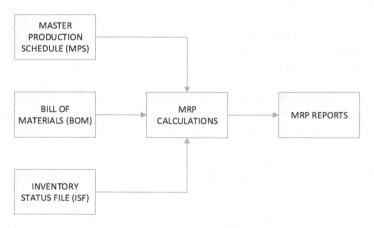

*Figure 14.1* Components of an MRP System

The MPS will usually contain a mix of both plans for customer ordered items and plans to produce in order to forecast sales. The forecast is a best estimate of what future demand will be, which may be derived from past sales and contact with the customer. These forecasts should be replaced by firm orders as the expected order date approaches. If actual orders exceed the forecast, then either the order will be delivered to the customer late or extra capacity must be obtained (for example, overtime, subcontracting) to meet the customer delivery date.

The mix of forecast and firm orders that a business can work to depends on the nature of the business. A resource-to-order company (such as a construction firm) will allocate resources and materials to a firm order only. Purchase-to-order organizations will not order materials until a firm order has been made but will have labour and equipment permanently available. A make-to-stock business, however, will work mainly to forecast demand.

## *Bill of materials*

The BOM identifies all the components required to produce a scheduled quantity of an assembly and the structure of how these components fit together to make that assembly. The BOM can be viewed as a product structure tree, similar to an organization chart (Figure 14.2). In this example, the item description is followed by the number of items required, in square brackets, and the item part number.

The final assembly of the product structure is denoted as level 0, while the structure is 'exploded' to further levels, representing subassemblies below this. These subassemblies are then broken down into further levels until the individual order components have been reached. Individual order components can be either a single component item or subassemblies purchased from suppliers and thus treated as a single component. The MRP system holds information on the number required of any item in the structure and the 'parent' item of which it is a component. Usually, the product structure is stored in a series of single-level BOMs, each of which holds a component part number and a list of the part numbers and quantities of the next lower level. The computer will move through all component BOMs in the product structure to derive a total number of components required for the product. Note that the same component may appear in different parts of the product structure if it is used more than once. What is needed is the total number required for each component to make the final assembly. The accuracy of the BOM is obviously vital in generating the correct schedule of parts at the right time.

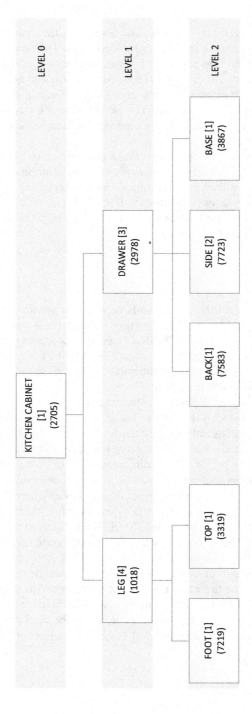

*Figure 14.2* BOM product structure

## *Inventory status file*

The BOM indicates the quantity of components needed from the product structure but this will not be directly translated into demand for components because it is likely that some of the components will be currently held in inventory. The inventory status file (ISF) provides information on the identification and quantity of items in stock. The MRP system will determine whether a sufficient quantity of an item is in stock or whether an order must be placed. The ISF will also contain the lead time, or time between order and availability, for each component.

As with the BOM, the accuracy of the ISF is vital, and some organizations use perpetual physical inventory checking to ensure that inventory records are accurate. This means a continuous check of inventory records against actual stock, instead of the traditional year-end checks for accounting purposes.

## *MRP Calculations*

The time-phased inventory status record can be used to show the inventory data requirements for each stock item and to follow the calculations necessary by the MRP programme. A simplified status record is shown in Table 14.1.

In this case, weekly time buckets have been used, which is usual for short-term plans. Longer time buckets may be used for long-term planning purposes. The definition of each row is as follows:

- Gross requirements: this row simply states the estimated requirements, in this case per week, for the item described. It is assumed that requirements occur during the time bucket (week) so that the scheduled receipts at the beginning of the week will cover them.
- Scheduled receipts: this row indicates when the item becomes available for use, from a previously released order. It is assumed that the item is received at the start of the time bucket period.

*Table 14.1* ISF showing net requirements

| Item: subassembly 1 | Week | | | | | |
|---|---|---|---|---|---|---|
| | *0* | *1* | *2* | *3* | *4* | *5* |
| Gross requirements | | 100 | 0 | 200 | 0 | 30 |
| Scheduled receipts | | | | 200 | | |
| Projected on Hand | 100 | 0 | 0 | 0 | 0 | −30 |
| New requirements | | | | | | 30 |
| Planned order release | | | | 30 | | |

- Projected on hand: numbers in this row show the number of units to be available at the end of each time bucket, which are based on the balance of requirements and receipts. The following is the formula for projected on hand:

Projected on hand = inventory on hand + scheduled receipts − gross requirements

- Net requirements: if the projected on hand is negative, it is called a net requirement and means that there will not be enough of this component to produce the quantities required to meet the master production schedule. Thus, when a negative projected on hand is shown, this will increase the net requirements row by a positive amount equal to the negative on hand.
- Planned order release (POR): the POR row indicates when an order should be released to ensure that the projected-on-hand figure does not become negative (that there are enough items to satisfy the MPS). The POR time must take into account the lead time between placing the order and the component becoming available (in the case of Table 14.1, the lead time is two weeks). Thus, the POR is offset by the required time amount to ensure that enough items are available to cover net requirements and sometimes to also cover net requirements in future time buckets. The MRP programme needs to work through all the levels of the assembly before calculating the net requirement for a time bucket, because the same item may be needed at different levels of the same assembly or in different assemblies.

### *MRP Reports*

A number of reports can be generated by the MRP programme, and they include information on the quantity of each item to order in the current and future time period, which is an indication of which due dates cannot be met and which shows when they can be met and shows changes to quantities of currently ordered items. The system can also show the results of simulation of scenarios for planning purposes. For instance, by entering a customer order into the master schedule, the effect of this extra work on overall customer due-date performance can be evaluated. If capacity restrictions mean that the order cannot be completed by the required due date, a new due date can be suggested.

## Manufacturing resource planning

MRP II extends the idea of MRP to other areas in the firm, such as marketing and finance. Thus, central databases hold information on product structure (the BOM file) that can be updated due to design changes – by engineering, for example. By incorporating financial elements into item details, inventory cost information can be used by finance departments. At a wider level, information provided by the MRP II system from simulations of business plans can be used to estimate plant investment needs and workforce requirements. This information can then be used to coordinate efforts across departments, including marketing, finance, engineering and manufacturing.

# 15 Supply chain management

The supply chain consists of the series of activities that moves materials from suppliers to operations to customers. Each product or service will have its own supply chain, which may involve many organizations in processing, transportation, warehousing and retail. The set of all relationships between a firm and its suppliers and customers for all of its supply chains is termed 'the supply network'. Activities on the input side to the organization are termed 'upstream' or 'supply' side and are divided into tiers of suppliers. Upstream suppliers that directly supply the organization are termed 'first tier'; suppliers that supply first-tier organizations are termed 'second tier'; and so on. Examples of upstream suppliers include component and subassembly suppliers. Activities on the output side are termed 'downstream' or 'demand' side and are divided into tiers of customers. Examples of downstream customers include wholesalers and retailers (see Chapter 5).

## Supply chain design

One of the key issues in supply chain design is that organizations need to cooperate with one another to achieve customer satisfaction. One of the reasons for that cooperation is to limit variability, which occurs in these networks and affects performance. There are a number of factors that increase variability in the supply chain. These include a time lag between ordering materials and getting them delivered to the customer. The use of order batching (when orders are not placed until they have reached a predetermined batch size) can also cause a mismatch between demand and order quantity. Price fluctuations such as price cuts and quantity discounts also lead to more demand variability in the supply chain as companies buy products before they need them. These effects can be amplified across the supply chain by a behaviour known as the bullwhip effect. The effect occurs when there is a lack of synchronization in supply chain members, when even a slight change in consumer sales will ripple backwards in the form of magnified oscillations in demand upstream. A number of steps can be taken to deal with the issue of variability in the supply chain. The traditional way to deal with uncertainty in demand is to improve forecast quality, but this is difficult to do in volatile markets, so there is an emphasis on reducing three critical lead times:

1    Time-to-market: how long does it take to recognize a market opportunity and bring products/services to the market?
2    Time-to-serve: how long does it take to capture a customer's order and to deliver the product?
3    Time-to-react: how long does it take to adjust the output of the business in response to volatile demand?

Another approach to reduce variability is to use smaller batch sizes in order to smooth the demand pattern. Batch sizes are large often because of the relatively high cost of each order. Technologies such as e-procurement and electronic data interchange (EDI) can reduce the cost of placing an order and so help eliminate the need for large batch orders. The use of a stable pricing policy can also help limit demand fluctuations.

## Agile and lean supply chains

Agile operations aim to respond quickly to market demand in order to retain current markets and gain new market share. As a strategy, agile operations can be seen to embrace uncertainty in markets and achieve competitive advantage through the flexibility and speed of their responses to them. The focus of agility has moved from an individual organization to supply chains, in which several companies work together. An alternative model to the agile supply chain is the concept of the lean supply chain. Lean supply chains adopt the concept of lean operations across the supply chain. Lean supply chains emphasize efficiency, which is achieved by policies such as minimizing inventory across the supply chain and continuous improvement across the supply chain. It has also been proposed that the lean and agile supply chain approaches can be combined by using the concept of leagility. Christopher and Towill (2001) propose three ways of bringing lean and agile together:

### Pareto rule (80/20 rule)

Of the volume in the supply chain, 80% is generated from 20% of the product line, so lean is used for 20% of predictable high-volume product lines to seek economies of scale and make to forecast. Use agile for the 80% of less predictable product lines, and aim for quick response and make to order (see Figure 15.1).

### Postponement

This involves using a decoupling point, which holds 'strategic' inventory in modular form until precise customer requirements are known. Companies can use lean methods up to the decoupling point and then agile methods beyond it (Figure 15.2). The concept can also be used with an information decoupling point. This represents the furthest point upstream at which 'real' demand information flows (i.e. information not distorted by policies such as reorder points). The point at which strategic inventory is held is also called

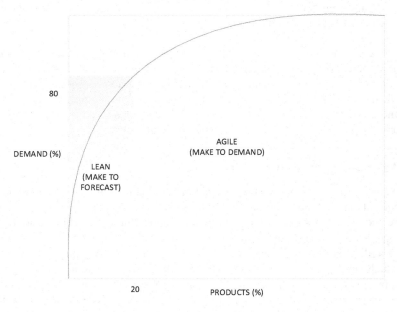

*Figure 15.1* Combining lean and agile by using the pareto rule

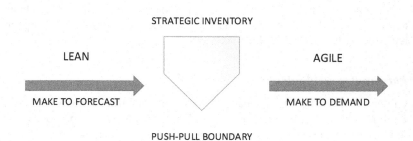

*Figure 15.2* Combining lean and agile by using postponement

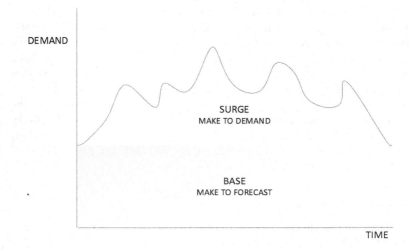

*Figure 15.3* Combining lean and agile by separating base and surge demand

the push-pull boundary as production is pushed up to the boundary point on the basis of forecast demand and then inventory is pulled from the boundary point on the basis of actual demand. A number of factors are considered when choosing the position in the supply chain at which the push-pull boundary should occur. These include the need to position the boundary before the proliferation of product or service designs and the need to ensure that the lead time after the boundary is relatively short in order to ensure fast responses to customer orders.

### Base and surge

Base demand can be forecast on the basis of history and so can be met by using lean to maximize efficiency. Surge demand is met by more flexible (agile) processes (Figure 15.3). One strategy is to source base demand in low-cost countries and meet surge demand in local markets (albeit at higher cost but more effective overall). This strategy is used in the fashion industry by such companies as Zara and Benetton.

## Supply chain integration

Organizations in a supply chain can have varying degrees of cooperation and integration. In order of increasing ownership, the options are a market relationship, strategic partnerships and alliances, virtual organization and vertical integration. At the level of an individual product or service, the amount of integration in the supply chain can be characterized as an analysis of the costs and risks in either making a component in-house or buying it from a supplier, termed a 'make-or-buy decision'. However, this approach does not take into account what may be critical strategic issues involved in deciding what it should do itself and what can be done by others. At a strategic level, supply chain integration decisions should be related to how the organization competes in the marketplace. For example, if speed of delivery is an order winner, then it may be necessary to make certain components in-house to ensure a fast and reliable supply. The different degrees of integration in the supply chain are now discussed.

## Market relationships

Cooperation can simply mean the act of conducting a transaction between two organizations. Here each purchase is treated as a separate transaction and the market relationship between the buyer and seller lasts as long as this transaction takes. This approach does have a number of advantages in that it permits flexibility, given that suppliers can be changed or discontinued if demand drops or a supplier introduces a new product. Other advantages include the use of competition between suppliers to improve performance in aspects such as price, delivery and quality. However, there can be disadvantages in this arrangement in that either side can end the relationship at any time. A supplier withdrawal requires the often-lengthy task of finding a new supplier. From a supplier perspective, the withdrawal of a buyer may cause a sudden drop in demand on the operations facility, leading to disruption and idle resources.

## Strategic partnerships and alliances

When an organization and supplier are trading successfully, they can decide to form a strategic alliance or strategic partnership. This involves a long-term relationship in which organizations work together and share information regarding aspects such as planning systems and developing products and processes. There may also be agreement on such aspects as product costs and product margins. The idea of a partnership or alliance is to combine the advantages of a marketplace relationship, and this combination encourages flexibility and innovation, with the advantages of vertical integration, which allows close coordination and control of such aspects as quality. From a supplier viewpoint, a long-term strategic partnership may give them the confidence to invest in resources and focus on a product line to serve a particular customer. Some factors may mitigate the formation of a partnership. For instance, for low-value items, the use of a partnership may not be worthwhile. Also, a company may not want to share sensitive information or lose control of a particular product or process.

### *The virtual organization*

The form of an organization's relationship within its supply chain is increasingly being affected by developments in e-business systems. E-business involves electronically mediated information exchanges, both within an organization and between organizations. The implications of e-business developments are that it becomes easier to outsource more and more supply chain activities to third parties and that the boundaries between and within organizations become blurred. This development is known as virtualization, and companies that follow this route are known as virtual organizations. The objective is that the absence of any rigid boundary or hierarchy within the organization should lead to a more responsive and flexible company with greater market orientation.

### *Vertical integration*

Complete integration is achieved by an organization when it takes ownership of other organizations in the supply chain. The amount of ownership of the supply chain by an organization is termed its 'level of vertical integration'. When an organization owns upstream or supply-side elements of the supply chain, it is termed 'backward vertical integration'. The ownership of downstream or demand-side elements in the supply chain is termed 'forward vertical integration'. When a company owns elements of a different supply chain, such as a holding company that has interests in organizations operating in various markets, the term used is 'horizontal integration'.

## Activities in the supply chain

In this section, supply chain activities are presented regarding the areas of procurement, which is the operations interface with upstream activities, and physical distribution management, which deals with downstream activities such as warehousing and transportation.

### *Procurement*

The role of procurement is to acquire all the materials needed by an organization in the form of purchases, rentals, contracts and other acquisition methods. The procurement process also includes activities such as selecting suppliers, approving orders and receiving goods from suppliers. The term 'purchasing' usually refers to the actual act of buying the raw materials, parts, equipment and all the other goods and services used in operations systems. However, the procurement process is often located in what is called the purchasing department.

Procurement is an important aspect of the operations function because the cost of materials can represent a substantial amount of the total cost of a product or service. There has recently been an enhanced focus on the procurement activity due to the increased use of process technology, in terms of both materials and information processing. In terms of materials processing, the use of process technology such as FMS has meant a reduction in labour costs and thus a further increase in the relative cost of materials associated with a manufactured product. This means that controlling the material costs becomes a major focus in the control of overall manufacturing costs for a product.

Before choosing a supplier, the organization must decide whether it is feasible and desirable to produce the good or service in-house. Buyers in purchasing departments, with assistance from operations, regularly perform a make-or-buy analysis to determine the source of supply. Often goods can be sourced internally at a lower cost, achieving higher quality or faster delivery than that from a supplier. On the other hand, suppliers who focus on delivering a good or service can specialize their expertise and resources and thus provide better performance. Strategic issues may also need to be considered when contemplating the outsourcing of supplies. For instance, internal skills required to offer a distinctive competence may be lost if certain activities are outsourced. It may also mean that distinctive competencies can be offered to competitors by the supplier. If a decision is made to use an external supplier, the next decision relates to the choice of that supplier. Criteria for choosing suppliers for quotation and approval include price, quality and delivery performance.

### *Physical distribution management*

Physical distribution management, sometimes called business logistics, refers to the movement of materials from the operation to the customer. Four of the main areas of physical distribution management are materials handling, warehousing, packaging and transportation.

Materials handling relates to the movement of materials, either within warehouses or between storage areas and transportation links. The aim of materials handling is to move materials as efficiently as possible. The types of materials handling systems available can be categorized as manual, mechanized and automated. A manual handling system relies on people to move material. This provides a flexible system, but it is feasible only when materials are movable by relying on people, with little assistance. An example is a supermarket where trolleys are used to assist with movement, but the presence of customers and the nature of the items make the use of mechanization or automation not feasible. Mechanized warehouses use equipment such as forklift trucks, cranes and conveyor systems to provide a more efficient handling system, which can also handle items too heavy for people. Automated warehouses use technology such as AGVs and loading/unloading machines to efficiently process high volumes of materials.

Not only are warehouses seen as long-term storage areas for goods, but they also provide a useful staging post for activities such as sorting, consolidating and packing goods for distribution along the supply chain.

Packaging provides a number of functions, including identifying the product, giving protection during transportation and storage, making handling easier and providing information to customers. The emphasis put on each of these factors will depend on the nature of the product, with protection being a major factor for some products. In terms of packaging materials, we have a choice that includes cardboard, plastic, glass, wood and metal. Which to choose among these depends on how each meets the functional needs of the product and on their relative cost.

Finally, transportation is an important element of the supply chain and can account for a substantial amount of the total costs of goods and services. The amount of the cost depends largely on the distance between the company and its customers and on the selected method of transportation. There are five main methods of transportation: rail, road, air, water and pipeline.

### *Last-mile delivery*

What is termed 'last-mile delivery' to customers can account for approximately 40% of total supply chain costs and so represents an important area of innovation. Companies wish to reduce these costs but have to meet customer demands for fast deliveries provided at a low price or for free. Issues in last-mile delivery include missed deliveries when the customer is not at home to receive the parcel, which means wasted time for both the courier and the customer. To address this issue, customer data is used to calculate the chance of a customer being home at a certain time. Alternatively, the use of GPS data can identify a customer's location rather than assigning a physical postcode address. Another strategy is to focus on important customers and provide them with enhanced services such as expedited shipping. Finally, reducing a courier's route by just 1 mile a day could bring large savings. Building a digital store of route directions and photos for visual reference to supplement the physical address can reduce travel times.

## Circular supply chains

The circular economy is a recent and important concept that involves decoupling economic activity from the consumption of finite resources and designing waste out of the system. The concept distinguishes between biological cycles, where biologically based materials such as food and wood can be fed back into the system through processes like composting, and technical cycles, which involve the restoration of products and materials through strategies such as reuse, repair or (ultimately) recycling. These concepts can be related to the supply chain in which circular supply chain management (CSCM) relates to the biological (regenerative) and technical (restorative) cycles on the basis of circular thinking. In general, supply chains can be classified into the following:

- Linear supply chains extract resources and dispose of packaging, products and associated waste at multiple stages of the supply chain.
- Closed-loop supply chains recover goods and packaging materials for the original producer. Waste is still generated in closed-loop supply chains, as it is rarely possible to reuse or recycle all unwanted items in the same supply chain.
- Circular supply chains aim to eliminate waste generated, by aiming to restore and regenerate resources in the industrial and natural ecosystem in which the supply chain is embedded.

## Reference

Christopher, M., and Towill, D. (2001) An integrated model for the design of agile supply chains. *International Journal of Physical Distribution and Logistics Management*, 31(4), pp. 235–46.

# 16  Project management

Projects are unique, one-time operations designed to accomplish a specific set of objectives in a limited time frame. Examples of projects include a building construction or introducing a new service or product to the market. In recent years, the ability to manage projects has become more important for operations managers. Increased global competition has led to the use of customized products serving niche markets. This expansion of product lines has led to the need for more project management of product and process development projects. Product life cycles have shortened, leading to the need to pay back project costs over less time, meaning the project management process must use fewer resources and minimize costs. Information-intensive products such as software and pharmaceuticals are generally costly to create but cheap to reproduce. The costs of these products are dominated by product and process development rather than the variable costs of production and distribution.

## Project management in the organization

Throughout the project, it is necessary to manage the three performance objectives of project management: time, cost and quality. The job of project managers is difficult since they are under pressure to meet quality performance measures under the constraints of a fixed timescale and fixed budget. They often need to make a compromise between project outcomes and the time and resources available. For example, if a customer wants a particular new product feature, then the cost and duration will need to increase; otherwise, other features will need to be omitted. Because of the unique nature of projects and the potentially high number of interrelated tasks involved, an effective way is needed to communicate project plans and progress across the project team. There are three main ways of structuring the organization of a project: project structure, functional structure and matrix structure. The reasons for choosing a particular structure are now discussed.

### The project structure

This consists of an organization that not only follows a team approach to projects but also has an organizational structure based on teams formed specifically for projects. The approach delivers a high focus on completing project objectives but can involve duplicating resources across teams, an inhibition of diffusion of learning across teams, a lack of hierarchical career structure and less continuity in employment. Many professional service firms, such as management consultancies, use this approach. With a functional structure, a project is given to the most appropriate functional department. Thus, the organizational structure remains in the standard hierarchical form. The approach ensures there is limited disruption to the normal organizational activities but can lead to a lack of focus on project objectives. A lack of coordination can result, especially if outside help is required. There can be a failure to meet customer needs if other departmental activities are taking priority over project work. With a matrix structure, project teams are overlaid on a functional structure in an effort to provide a balance between functional and project needs. There are three different forms of matrix structures: the functional matrix, in which a project manager reports to functional heads to coordinate staff across departments; a balanced matrix, in which the project manager manages the project jointly with functional heads; and a project matrix, in which functional staff join a project team for a fixed period of time.

## Project management activities

Projects require a clear definition and boundary to determine what should be inside and what should be outside the scope of the project. Scoping the project is crucial when outsourcing, because disputes can occur if the project does not have a clear definition. Definition may be made through a detailed evaluation at the start of the project or may evolve through a process of interaction with the customer during development. After the project definition phase has been completed, the project management process will feature the following main elements: estimating, planning and control.

### Project estimating

At the start of the project, a broad plan is drawn up that assumes unlimited resources. Once project estimates have been made of the resources required to undertake these activities, it is possible to compare overall project requirements with available resources. If highly specialized resources are required, then the project completion date may have to be set to ensure that these resources are not overloaded. This is a resource-constrained project.

Alternatively, there may be a need to complete a project in a specific time frame (for example, a due date specified by customer). In this case, alternative resources may have to be used (for example, subcontractors) to ensure that the project is completed on time. This is a time-constrained project.

The next step is to generate estimates for the time and resources required to undertake each task defined in the project. This information can then be used to plan what resources are required and what activities should be undertaken over the life cycle of the project. Once the activities have been identified and their resource requirements estimated, it is necessary to define their relationship to one another. There are some activities that can begin only once other activities have been completed. This is termed a 'serial relationship'. Other activities may be totally independent, and thus, they have a parallel relationship. For a reasonably sized project, there may be a range of alternative plans that may meet the project objectives. Project management software can be used to assist in choosing the most feasible schedule, by recalculating resource requirements and timings for each operation.

### Project planning

The purpose of the project planning stage is to ensure that the project objectives of cost, time and quality are met. It does this by estimating both the level and timing of resources needed over the project's duration. These steps may need to be undertaken repeatedly in a complex project due to uncertainties and to accommodate changes as the project progresses. The project management method uses a systems approach to deal with a complex task in that the components of the project are broken down repeatedly into smaller tasks until a manageable chunk is defined. Each task is given its own cost, time and quality objectives. It is then essential that responsibility is assigned to achieving these objectives for each particular task. This procedure should produce a work breakdown structure (WBS), which shows the hierarchical relationship between the project tasks. A typical WBS will have at the top level the project and at the bottom level the individual work package. A work package is an individual work element that can be accurately defined, budgeted, scheduled and controlled. Between the top and bottom levels, various categories can be defined. These categories are usually organized in a product-oriented fashion but may be task oriented for service operations such as design or management.

### Project control

Project control involves monitoring the project objectives of cost, time and quality as the project progresses. It is important to monitor and assess performance as the project progresses so that the project does not deviate from plans to a large extent. Milestones or time events are defined during the project when performance against objectives can be measured. The amount of control depends on the size of the project. Larger projects require developing control activities from the project leader to team leaders. Computer project management packages can be used to automate the collection of project progress data and the production of progress reports.

## Network analysis

Network analysis refers to the use of network-based techniques for analysing and managing projects. This section describes two network analysis techniques of the critical path method (CPM) and the project evaluation and review technique (PERT).

### *Critical path method*

Critical path diagrams are used extensively to show the activities undertaken during a project and the dependencies between these activities. There are two methods of constructing critical path diagrams: activity on arrow (AOA), where the arrows represent the activities, and activity on node (AON), where the nodes represent the activities. For the AON notation, each activity task is represented by a node with the format in Figure 16.1.

Thus, a completed network will consist of a number of nodes connected by lines, one for each task, between a start node and an end node. Once the network diagram has been constructed, it is possible to follow a sequence of activities, called a path, through the network, from start to end. The length of time it takes to follow the path is the sum of all the durations of activities on that path. The path with the longest duration determines the project

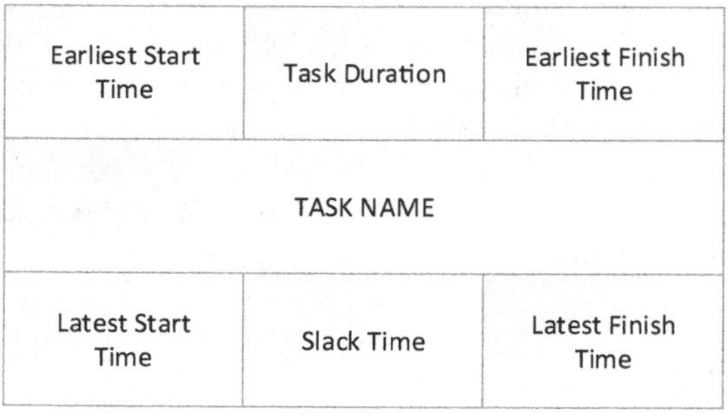

| Earliest Start Time | Task Duration | Earliest Finish Time |
|---|---|---|
| | TASK NAME | |
| Latest Start Time | Slack Time | Latest Finish Time |

*Figure 16.1* CPM AON notation

completion time. This is called the critical path, because any change in duration in any activities on this path will cause the whole project duration to become either shorter or longer.

Although network diagrams are ideal for showing the relationship between project tasks, they do not provide a clear view of which tasks are being undertaken over time and particularly how many tasks may be undertaken in parallel at any one time. The Gantt chart provides an overview for the project manager, to allow them to monitor project progress against planned progress, so it provides a valuable information source for project control.

### *Project evaluation and review technique*

The PERT approach attempts to take into account the fact that most task durations are not fixed but instead vary when they are executed. Thus, PERT provides a way of incorporating risk into project schedules. It does this by using a beta probability distribution to describe the variability inherent in the processes. The probabilistic approach involves three time estimates for each activity:

1   Optimistic time: the task duration under the most optimistic conditions.
2   Pessimistic time: the task duration under the most pessimistic conditions.
3   Most likely time: the most likely task duration.

To derive the average or expected time for a task duration, the following equation is used:

Expected duration = [optimistic + (4 x most likely) + pessimistic]/6

Greater risk is reflected in the spread between optimistic and most likely and in particular between most likely and pessimistic. For an activity with no risk, the values of optimistic, most likely and pessimistic would be the same.

# 17 Quality

Quality is one of the five performance objectives, and having a high-quality product or service often represents an essential element when being considered by the customer. Quality is a particular challenge for service organizations in that both the tangible and intangible aspects of the service (for example, the food and the service at a restaurant) must meet quality standards in order to earn repeat customers.

## Defining quality

Quality can actually mean quite different things to different people. This section starts by looking at different perspectives of what we mean by quality. Most definitions of quality, in the context of business, recognize the role of the customer in judging the quality of a product or service, so we look at the dimensions that customers may use in judging the quality of products and services. Garvin (1988) provides a model that presents five perspectives on a definition of quality:

1    Transcendent: this views quality as excellence or the best available. An Aston Martin sports car or a seven-star hotel would wish to be seen in this way. This view implies that customers will be able to recognize excellence when they see it.
2    Product based: this views quality as a precise and measurable variable that is made up of a number of characteristics. This implies quality can be measured as a number of attributes making up a product or service. Thus, the quality of a car could be measured by its acceleration, top speed, engine size, etc. The assessment of product variables may vary considerably among individuals.
3    User based: this views quality as the level of satisfaction held by an individual customer. This implies that quality is a subjective concept and will vary depending on the needs of individual customers – for

example, a car with a wide range of options for engine sizes and accessories that can be customized to an individual customer's needs. Quality in this view is defined as how well the product performs its intended function according to the customer.

4 Operations based: this views quality as conformance to internally developed specifications in service operations or manufacturing. This implies that quality will be defined in terms of productivity targets. Thus, a car produced consistently over time with no defective components and matching the design specification would be considered of high quality.

5 Value based: this views quality in terms of best price for a given purpose. This implies quality is viewed from a customer perspective in terms of value for money. Thus, a quality product is seen to be as useful as competing products but cheaper or offering greater satisfaction than products sold at a comparable price.

These five perspectives demonstrate that there is no single 'correct' view of how to define quality, and all of these perspectives may be relevant but have their limitations if taken in isolation. Slack et al. (2016) attempt to reconcile these different views with the following definition of quality: quality is consistent conformance to customers' expectations.

'Consistent' implies that conformance to specification is not an ad hoc event; instead, the product or service delivery process has been designed so that the product or service meets the specification by using a set of measurable characteristics (product-based view). 'Conformance' implies that there is a need to meet a clear specification (operations-based view). 'Customers' expectations' implies that the customer receives a product or service with attributes that they can reasonably expect (user based) at a reasonable cost (value based).

## Measuring quality

For services, the assessment of quality is made during the service delivery process. The nature of services in terms of their intangibility, the fact that they often involve customer contact and the customized nature of professional services means that defining quality is difficult. One approach to the definition of quality in services is given by Parasuraman et al. (1985) as five principal dimensions that customers use to judge service quality:

1 *Reliability* is related to the ability to perform a service dependably and accurately. Customers expect reliable service – that is, a service that is delivered on time, in the same manner and without errors every time.

2   *Responsiveness* is related to the willingness to help customers and to provide prompt service. Customers particularly dislike waiting for a service, especially if there is no apparent reason for the wait. A quick recovery after a service failure occurs is also important in achieving a favourable customer experience.

3   *Assurance* is related to the abilities of employees delivering a service to the customer. They should demonstrate competence, respect for the customer and an ability to effectively communicate with the customer.

4   *Empathy* is also related to the abilities of employees; to their providing a caring, individualized service that requires their approachability and sensitivity; and to their demonstrating an effort to understand the customer's needs.

5   *Tangibles* are related to the physical aspects of the service delivery environment, such as the condition of the physical surroundings. Clean and tidy physical surroundings provide the customer with evidence of the care and attention to detail shown by the service provider.

The concept is that customers use these five dimensions to form their judgements of service quality, which are based on a comparison between expectations and perceptions of that service quality. These measurements are gathered by using the survey research instrument SERVQUAL (Parasuraman et al., 1988). The difference between the expected and perceived service level is termed the 'service quality gap' and can be used to identify areas for improvement in service-quality.

## Improving quality

This section covers methods for organization-wide quality improvement. The methods covered are the quality gaps model, total quality management (TQM), six-sigma quality and statistical process control (SPC).

### *The quality gaps model*

This section will cover the customer-oriented quality improvement technique of the quality gap approach. The approach was developed by Parasuraman et al. (1985) to devise a way of improving quality by identifying the gap between what customers expect from a service and what they perceive they are actually getting. The difference between the two is termed the 'quality gap', and the size of this gap determines customer dissatisfaction. Although the concept was originally devised for service operations, it can be used to assess quality failures in manufactured products. There are five possible quality gaps in the model (Figure 17.1).

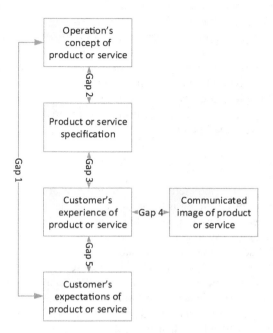

*Figure 17.1* The quality gaps model

The gaps are described in turn:

Gap 1: operation's concept of product or service – customer's expectations of product or service. This is when the operation's concept of the product or service does not meet customer expectations. For example, a customer may expect a breakfast as part of their hotel room booking, but it is not included in the specification. This gap can be closed by operations gaining a close understanding of customer expectations of the product or service.

Gap 2: operation's concept of product or service – product or service specification. This is when the operation's concept of the product or service is not followed by the product or service specification. This could be due to a poorly detailed product specification or a lack of detailed plans for undertaking the service delivery process. For example, the concept of a luxury hotel could be undermined by a poorly defined room-cleaning process. This gap can be closed by ensuring the product or service specification is aligned with the concept.

Gap 3: customer's experience of product or service – product or service specification. This is when there is a gap between the customer's experience of a product or service and the service specification. For example, a customer requests a quiet room in a hotel and is given a room with a connecting door to the adjacent room, which permits noise to travel. This service failure could be due to poor staff training in room allocation or a lack of resources – that is, room availability. This gap can be closed by ensuring that the product or service specification is actually met.

Gap 4: customer's experience of product or service – communicated image of product or service. This is when there is a gap between the customer's experience of a product or service and claims made in any promotional activity concerning that product or service. For example, promotional material for a hotel shows pictures of fitness equipment that is only available to hotel guests for a fee. This gap can be closed by making sure promotional materials do not imply a level of service that is not available.

Gap 5: customer's experience of product or service – customer's expectations of product or service. This is when there is a gap between a customer's experience of a product or service and their expectation of that product or service. This gap is a consequence of gaps 1 to 4 and can be closed by identifying and closing the other relevant gaps. For example, a customer may be disappointed at the size of their 'large' hotel room. Their expectation of what constitutes a 'large' hotel room size could have been affected by their previous experience of similar hotels or the same chain of hotels (gap 1), incorrectly specified room sizes when the hotel was designed (gap 2), incorrect allocation of a family to a standard room (gap 3) or images on the hotel website that give a false impression of room size (gap 4).

### Total quality management

TQM is a philosophy and approach that aims to ensure that high quality, as defined by the customer, is a primary concern throughout the organization and that all parts of the organization work towards this goal. Total quality management does not prescribe a number of steps that must be followed to achieve high quality but rather should be considered a framework within which organizations can work. The TQM process will depend on factors such as customer needs, employee skills and the current state of quality management in the organization.

TQM has evolved over a number of years from ideas presented by several experts in the field, known as quality gurus. Oakland (2003) sees the approaches of the quality gurus as essentially complementary and has suggested his own 11-step process. The main principles of TQM covered in these plans can be summarized in the following three statements:

1   Customers define quality, and thus, their needs must be met. Earlier, it was stated that the organization must consider quality from both the producer and the customer points of view. Thus, the product design must take into consideration the production process so that the design specification can be met. A customer perspective is required so that the implications for customers are considered at all stages in corporate decision-making.
2   It is a principle of TQM that the responsibility for quality should rest with the people undertaking the tasks that can either directly or indirectly affect the quality of customer service. It requires not only a commitment to avoid mistakes but actually a capability to improve how they undertake their jobs. This requires management to adopt an approach of empowerment. It also involves providing people with training and the decision-making authority necessary so that they can take responsibility for the work they are involved in and learn from their experiences.
3   An attitude of continuous improvement must be developed and then emphasized to instil a culture that recognizes how important quality is to performance.

### Six-sigma quality

Six sigma is a quality improvement initiative launched by Motorola in the United States in the 1980s. The initiative was originally conceived by Motorola to achieve quality levels that are within six-sigma control limits, corresponding to a rate of 3.4 defective parts per million (PPM). However, six sigma has developed beyond a defect-elimination programme to become a company-wide initiative to reduce costs through process efficiency and increase revenues through process effectiveness.

A five-step method of define, measure, analyse, improve and control (DMAIC) is used for improving both process performance and process or product design. The DMAIC method emphasizes using statistical tools to gather data at each of the five stages: define, measure, analyse, improve and control.

1   Define: identify a potential area of improvement and define the project scope and processes involved. Assign a project team.
2   Measure: decide which characteristics of the process require improvement. Identify the critical input variables that can be controlled and that

affect the output. Define what constitutes unacceptable performance or a defect. Collect sufficient data on process performance.

3    Analyse: use the data collected in the measure phase to document current performance. Use control charts to judge whether the process is in control. The process performance can be benchmarked against similar internal or external processes.

4    Improve: eliminate the root causes of non-random variation to achieve improvements in predictability, dispersion and centring. If no special causes can be found, the improvement effort may need to focus on the design of the product or process.

5    Control: verify and embed the change through the use of techniques such as control charts. Share experiences to transfer knowledge between process improvement teams.

To summarize, the six-sigma approach emphasizes a measurable improvement in revenues through increasing effectiveness and efficiency. It uses the DMAIC method to ensure that process improvement efforts are based on factual data. It uses customer-focused improvements to ensure that change increases revenue and uses training to ensure that the appropriate tools are used for specific improvement projects.

### *Statistical process control*

SPC is an operation-oriented technique for quality improvement. It involves taking a sample that checks the quality of an item that is engaged in a process. Thus, SPC should be seen as a quality check for a process rather than as a product design. Statistical process control works by identifying the nature of variations in a process, which are classified as being caused by *chance* causes or *assignable* causes.

All processes have some inherent variability, due to factors such as ambient temperature, wear from moving parts or slight variations in the composition of the material that is being processed. The technique of SPC involves calculating the limits of these chance-cause variations for a stable system, so that any problems with the process can be identified quickly. The limits of the chance causes of variations are called control limits and are shown on a control chart, which also shows sample data of the measured characteristic over time. There are control limits above and below the target value for the measurement, termed the 'upper control limit' (UCL) and 'lower control limit' (LCL) respectively. An example control chart is shown in Figure 17.2.

The behaviour of the process can thus be observed by studying the control chart. If the sample data plotted on the chart shows a random pattern in

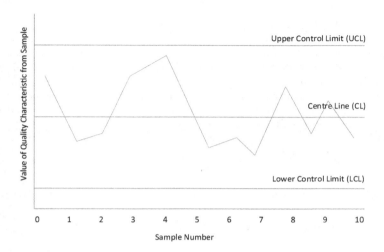

*Figure 17.2* SPC chart

the UCL and LCL, then the process is *in control*. However, if a sample falls outside the control limits or the plot shows a non-random pattern, then the process is *out of control*.

If an out-of-control process is discovered, then it is assumed to have been caused by an assignable cause of variation. This is a variation in the process that is not due to random variation but instead can be attributed to some change in the process, and it needs to be investigated and rectified. However, in some instances, the process could actually be working properly and the results could have been caused by the UCL:

Type I error: an error is indicated from the sample output when none actually occurs.

Type II error: an error is occurring but has not been indicated by the sample output.

Thus, type I errors may lead to some costly but unnecessary investigation and rectification work. They may even lead to an unnecessary recall of 'faulty' products. Type II errors will lead to defective products as a result of an out-of-control process going unnoticed. Customer compensation and a loss of sales may result if defective products reach the marketplace. The sampling method should ensure that the probability of type I and type II errors is kept as low as reasonably possible.

## References

Garvin, D.A. (1988) *Managing Quality*, Free Press.

Oakland, J.S. (2003) *TQM: Text with Cases*, 3rd edn., Butterworth Heinemann.

Parasuraman, A., Zeithaml, V.A., and Berry, L.L. (1985) A conceptual model of service quality and its implications for future research. *Journal of Marketing*, 49(4), pp. 41–50.

Parasuraman, A., Zeithaml, V.A., and Berry, L.L. (1988) SERVQUAL: a multiple item scale for measuring customer perceptions of service quality. *Journal of Retailing*, 64(1), pp. 12–40.

Slack, N., Brandon-Jones, A., and Johnston, R. (2016) *Operations Management*, 8th edn., Pearson Education Limited.

# 18 Performance measurement and improvement

In this chapter traditional measures of performance, such as productivity and efficiency, are covered, and then measures associated with operations' five performance objectives are discussed. The next step is to compare each performance measure against a performance standard in order to identify areas for improvement. Once priorities for improvement have been identified, an improvement programme can be implemented. In this chapter, the improvement approaches of business process management (BPM), business process re-engineering (BPR) and continuous improvement (CI) are discussed.

## How do we measure performance?

Performance measurement involves both choosing the measures that will be used to identify where improvements should take place and determining whether improvement has taken place after the change has been implemented. Traditionally, performance measures in operations have focused on indicators such as productivity, which divides the value of the output by the value of the input resources consumed, and efficiency, which relates to the use of a resource in terms of availability. Operations strategy considers that the focus of improvement should be directed towards appropriate areas of the operation where any increase in performance will help the organization meet its strategic goals. In this text, the five performance objectives – quality, speed, dependability, flexibility and cost – are used to measure operations performance in relation to its strategy. It also shows that strategies that rely on immediate cost-cutting (achieving economy by lowering the costs of inputs into the operations transformation process) should be replaced by strategies that aim to improve performance on the other performance objectives, which will then lead to a reduction in cost.

### The SCOR model

The supply chain operations reference (SCOR) model provides a framework for measuring and evaluating the performance of supply chain processes.

Measurements are made of five key processes that are undertaken along the supply chain by all participating organizations. These processes are defined as plan, source, make, deliver and return.

- 'Plan' means managing the customer-supplier links in the supply chain to ensure that the supply chain strategy aligns requirements with the resources available.
- 'Source' means managing procurement activities and ensuring that suppliers are selected, deliveries scheduled and inventories managed.
- 'Make' means managing the transformation process that adds value to products and services.
- 'Deliver' means managing order fulfilment and transporting goods to the customer.
- 'Return' means managing customer returns and other post-delivery customer support.

The SCOR model incorporates benchmarking activities to indicate where performance should be improved and a SCOR roadmap to provide a framework for implementation – that is, how performance should be improved.

## Where should we improve performance?

To identify where performance improvement should take place, it is necessary to compare the performance measure against a performance standard. This standard can be internal to the organization, such as comparing against previous performance or against targets for future performance. Internal targets are often based on a comparison between past financial and sales performance and targets for future performance. The advantage of these measures is that they are widely used, are comparable across organizations and use data that are readily available. However, they may be of limited value in identifying why performance is above or below a target value. External targets include comparisons with competitor performance, best practice or best-in-class performance or market requirements. External performance targets have the advantage of providing a comparison of performance against competitors operating in similar competitive markets. This approach is often called benchmarking and is described later in this chapter.

In terms of the measures associated with the five operations performance objectives, two models can be used to identify where performance should be improved. The Hill method (Hill and Hill, 2012) is based on market requirements. The concepts of order winning and qualifying factors are used to distinguish between those factors that directly contribute to winning business and those that are necessary to qualify for the customer's consideration between a range of products/services (see Chapter 2). The second model uses a combination of market and competitive factors and two dimensions – importance and performance – to help operations managers prioritize performance objectives (see Slack et al., 2016).

## *Benchmarking*

'Benchmarking' can be defined as the continual measurement of an organization's products and processes against a company recognized as a leader in that industry. Analysing competitor products is an older technique, which forms part of the product design process. Benchmarking was initially restricted to the comparison of direct competitors in the manufacturing sector. Now it is practised in the service sector (for example, banks), in all functional areas (for example, marketing) and in comparison with a wide variety of competitors from which lessons can be learnt (not just the best in class). Because of the widespread use of the technique and the requests by many organizations to visit the same high-performance firms, much benchmarking data is held in databases for general use. A number of models for implementing a benchmarking programme have been developed. The following is a summary of the main activities involved in benchmarking:

- Planning: understand the business's processes; identify key processes; and form benchmarking teams.
- Analysis: conduct research on possible competitors, and formulate questions to elicit the required information. Establish a relationship with a partner organization, and collect and share information.
- Implementation: implement and monitor improvements suggested by the analysis.

The relevant processes in the organization need to be benchmarked before comparing them with those of a competitor. Processes are benchmarked in terms of metrics (numeric measurements) and procedures (process flows). For example, a payment process could be measured by the time taken from receiving the request to delivering the payment. The technique would also measure the type and amount of personnel involved in each step of the process. Two problems with some benchmarking programmes have been the focus on developing metrics and the lack of energy put into implementing changes suggested by the benchmarking process. Other problems include the difficulty in obtaining competitor information and the fact that if the process is used simply to emulate a competitor, competitive advantage may be short-lived as the competitor makes further improvements.

## How do we improve performance?

Three performance improvement approaches are covered here: BPM, BPR and CI.

### *Business process management*

BPM refers to the analysis and improvement of business processes. A process is a set of activities designed to produce a desired output from a specified input. The process orientation matches the idea of the main objectives of the operations function as the management of the transformation process of inputs (resources) into outputs (goods and services), covered in Chapter 1. Although BPM is usually used in the broad sense, it is also used more narrowly to refer to software technologies for automating the management of specific processes. In its widest sense, however, BPM brings together aspects such as the following:

- Process-mapping techniques, such as process mapping and service blueprinting.
- Simulation modelling techniques, such as BPS.
- Implementation of information technologies, such as workflow systems.
- Improvement approaches, such as BPR.
- Assessment models, such as ISO9000.

### *Business process re-engineering*

In the early to mid 1990s, organization-wide transformational change was advocated under the label of BPR. It was popularized through the pronouncements of Hammer and Champy (1993) and Davenport (1993). The essence of BPR is the assertion that business processes, organizational structures, team structures and employee responsibilities can be fundamentally altered to improve business performance. A five-step approach to the introduction of BPR was suggested by Davenport (1993).

1   Identify processes for innovation. The organization should select a process or processes that are critical to the organization and provide a potentially large increase in performance in return for the re-engineering effort. The scope and number of process redesign projects must be compatible with the organization's ability and experience to undertake them.
2   Identify change levers. The three main enablers or levers of change are IT, information and organizational/human resources.

   Much information is not manipulated by IT resources in the organization but may still be a powerful lever in making process innovation possible. Examples include the visible display of information on the shop floor in lean production organizations and the market information used by executives in making strategic decisions. For example, many process innovations will lead to increased worker empowerment, which may require an adjustment in organizational culture to ensure successful implementation. Successfully using teams is also essential in implementing cross-functional processes.

3 Develop process vision. The process innovation effort must be consistent with the organization's strategy. A process vision consists of measurable objectives and provides the link between strategy and action. A shared vision is essential to ensuring true innovation, rather than standard improvement efforts such as simplification and rationalization. A vision allows conventional wisdom about how processes are undertaken to be questioned. Key activities in developing a process vision include assessing an existing business strategy for process direction, consulting with process customers, benchmarking process performance targets and developing process performance objectives and attributes.

4 Understand existing processes. This step is necessary to enable those involved in the innovation activities to develop a common understanding of the existing processes, understand complexities, avoid duplicating current problems and provide a benchmark against which to measure improvement. Traditional process-oriented approaches such as flow charting can be used for this task but do not contain the elements necessary to implement radical change.

5 Design and prototype the new processes. The design of new processes requires a team with a mix of members who can deliver creative and innovative process solutions and ensure that they are implemented. Key activities in the design and prototype phase are brainstorming design activities, assessing the feasibility of these alternatives, prototyping the new process design, developing a migration strategy and implementing the new organizational structure and systems. Business Process Simulation (Chapter 8) can be a valuable tool in assessing a new process design.

### Continuous improvement

CI programmes are associated with incremental changes in the organization, and their cumulative effect is to deliver an increased rate of performance improvement. CI is associated with the JIT and lean philosophy, where it is referred to as 'kaizen', a Japanese term meaning a way of getting to the ideals of JIT by a continuous stream of improvements over time.

CI is also associated with the concept of the learning organization, which aims to create an environment that builds knowledge in the organization and can use that to improve performance. The need for organizational learning has been identified as a consequence of the need for organizations to continually produce innovations in order to maintain a competitive edge. The ability to generate a continuous stream of ideas for improvement and then to implement them is seen as a sustainable competitive advantage for organizations. To consider how an organization learns is really to consider how people in that organization learn and how the results of that learning are integrated into the practices, procedures and processes of the organization. The transfer of knowledge from an individual to an organizational system means that the knowledge becomes independent of the individual and is possessed by the organization and replicable by individuals in that organization. The concept of knowledge management overlaps that of organizational learning but may be distinguished from it by a greater focus on the management of knowledge as a strategic asset and an emphasis on encouraging the sharing of knowledge.

CI requires creating the right environment in which the importance of the approach is recognized and rewarded. This means ensuring the involvement of all the members of the organization and ensuring that these members have the problem-solving skills necessary to achieve worthwhile improvements. The issues of environment, involvement and problem-solving skills will now be explored in relation to implementing CI. To create the right environment in which improvement can take place, it is important to have a set of procedures for the improvement process, which formalizes actions so that progress can be monitored and measured. A procedure for an improvement study could follow the steps of the plan-do-check-act (PDCA) cycle (Figure 18.1) as follows:

PLAN      What changes are needed to gain continual improvement?
DO        Analyse appropriate data. Carry out suggested changes to the process.
CHECK     Evaluate the results of the changes to the process.
ACT       Make the changes permanent, or try another step (go to step 1).

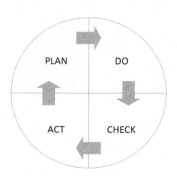

*Figure 18.1* The PDCA cycle

The PDCA cycle was developed for improving production processes and separates the process creation and execution phases (plan and do) from the process checking and improvement (check and act) phases. Thus, a continuous feedback loop is created between process operation and process improvement.

## References

Davenport, T.H. (1993) *Process Innovation: Re-engineering Work Through Information Technology*, Harvard Business School Press.

Hammer, M., and Champy, J. (1993) *Re-engineering the Corporation: A Manifesto for Business Revolution*, Harper Business.

Hill, A. and Hill, T. (2018) *Operations Strategy: Design, Implementation and Delivery*, Red Globe Press.

Slack, N., Brandon-Jones, A., and Johnston, R. (2016) *Operations Management*, 8th edn., Pearson Education Limited.

# Index

Printed in the United States
by Baker & Taylor Publisher Services